Balancing Act

TEACH

COACH

MENTOR

INSPIRE

Dr. Andrew Temte, CFA

© 2021 Andrew Temte

Published by Kaplan Publishing, a division of Kaplan, Inc.
750 Third Avenue
New York, NY 10017

10 9 8 7 6 5 4 3 2 1

ISBN: 978-1-5062-7664-9

Kaplan Publishing print books are available at special quantity discounts to use for sales promotions, employee premiums, or educational purposes. For more information or to purchase books, please call the Simon & Schuster special sales department at 866-506-1949.

About the Author

As President and Global Head of Corporate Learning, Dr. Andrew Temte, CFA, spearheads Kaplan's efforts in helping employees remain relevant in the future world of work as well as in helping companies continuously improve by attracting the right talent and upskilling/reskilling their workforce. In this capacity, he oversees and leverages assets, capabilities, and talent across Kaplan's global footprint.

A thought leader on issues related to professional education and workforce skilling, Dr. Temte has been published and cited in a number of media outlets. Previously, Dr. Temte served in the following professional positions: CEO of Kaplan Professional, Dean of the Kaplan University School of Professional and Continuing Education, Interim President of Mount Washington College, and President of the Kaplan University College of Business and Technology. This blend of higher education and professional education experience gives Dr. Temte a unique perspective over the issues surrounding the future of employment and workplace relevance.

Dr. Temte started his professional education career in 1990, working with Dr. Carl Schweser to build the Schweser Study Program into the leader in CFA exam review. Under Dr. Temte's direction, Kaplan Schweser became a leading global provider of innovative, efficient, and effective financial education solutions.

Dr. Temte earned his doctorate in finance from the University of Iowa with a concentration in international finance and investment theory. He holds the CFA designation and has over fourteen years of university teaching experience in the areas of corporate finance, investments, and international finance.

Dedication

When I planted the initial seeds for this work in 2017, the goal was to compile a series of "Tales from a Mid-level Senior Executive" to describe the challenges and opportunities that face leaders who must manage up, down, and across complex organizations. As the cornerstones were laid, it quickly became apparent that the concept of *balance* was the thread that tied my personal and professional stories together.

I'm grateful for the opportunities I've had to cross paths with some extraordinary people throughout my life and am thankful to current and former colleagues, business partners, and friends for the small but significant parts they've played in shaping the leader and individual I am today. I've used the tapestry we painted through our interactions to learn and grow. I'm particularly thankful for the role my mentors and coaches have played in my development—specifically Carl Schweser, Dan Johnson-Wilmot, Keith Sherony, Roger Leithold, and Mike Marsh.

In most book dedications, there are references to family, and this one is no exception. I'd like to thank my dad, Bill, for nailing the basement window shut when I was seventeen; my mom, Louise, for trying (in vain) to get me to learn the piano; my sons, Nick and Brandon, for showing me what true, unconditional love means; and my wife, Linda, for being my polar opposite, my "Sol Mate," and continually challenging me to become that next best version of myself.

I am truly blessed.

Contents

Introduction

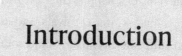

Success without balance is often more disastrous than failure with balance.

When the unbalanced achieve victory, it often serves to further destructive habits. When the balanced suffer defeat, resilience and perseverance grows.

As a young boy in primary school, I was a picture of academic success. Most subjects came easily to me, which made me the odd boy out. In third and fourth grades, one teacher literally sent me out of class for being too far ahead. While my peers studied in the classroom, I sat outside drawing pictures on a canvas the custodian had set up in the hallway to help me pass the time.

In junior high school, I was a straight-A student, a charter member of the La Crosse BoyChoir, president of the student council, and a competitive member of the football, wrestling, and track teams. As viewed through the lens of the adults around me, I was on the "right" path and perfectly positioned to move forward.

Two things happened in my midteens that completely disrupted that path, as they have the paths of many promising adolescents before and after me: one was rock 'n' roll, the other was drugs and alcohol.

I joined my first rock band in the eighth grade, and we played our first gigs at homecomings, winter carnivals, and junior proms throughout western Wisconsin and southeastern Minnesota. Suddenly, the eleventh-grade girls were "seeing" this eighth grader for the first time, and I soon realized that there was more to life than just being the smartest person in the room.

Pursuing music meant partying with older kids, and partying with older kids meant delving into the world of drugs and alcohol at a relatively young age. I was at the top of my class, being labeled "special," "gifted," and "talented." However, that was nothing compared to the allure and ego stroke of performing in front of a live crowd, not to mention getting the attention and affection of older students.

By the time I reached the eleventh grade, I was at a crossroads. I had already completed most of the coursework required to gain admission to college, but at that point, the State of Wisconsin had no mechanism for advancing those they labeled "gifted." Skipping grades and gaining early admission wasn't a straightforward option or a well-worn path.

Instead, the two options I saw in front of me were either spending another year of my life passing time until graduation or dropping out of school and diving headfirst into a world of drugs, sex, and rock 'n' roll. I was seventeen years old at the time—which do you think I chose?

Against the better wishes of my parents, teachers, and just about every adult around me, I dropped out of school in the eleventh grade and went off to pursue my rock 'n' roll fantasy.

What I failed to acknowledge at the time was that being a rock star—selling music for a living—wasn't just a lifestyle; it was a business. Having the musical ability, as I foolishly believed at the time, wasn't enough. To succeed, I also needed financial, behavioral, managerial, and marketing skills.

Unless you're an extraordinary talent or have an "in" within the industry—such as an established rock star or a music executive in the family—it was a very business-like grind. Since I had dropped out of school, I didn't have such skills and capabilities in my portfolio.

For the next four years, from 1980 to 1984, I traveled with my band, Cry Wolf, across the upper Midwest, bouncing from small-town bar to small-town bar, spending what little money we earned on food, travel, and the next high. I thought the rock star lifestyle was all about freedom and never having to work a day in your life, but it turned out to be the exact opposite.

Every Tuesday morning, we'd travel to whatever town we were playing in that week, spend three or four hours setting up our equipment, and play in front of a small audience every night through the weekend. Then at the end of the week, we'd pack it all up and head home for a few days, only to do it all over again the next week—at least on the weeks when we were lucky enough to have a few days off in between.

It was a difficult way to live. It was ultimately for the love of a girl that I decided to give it all up in 1984. That, and waking up in a pool of my own blood.

Linda had taken a liking to me very early on in high school, despite the fact that she was dating my best friend at the time. When we finally reconnected at age twenty-one, on the Sunday after Thanksgiving of 1984, I was already questioning my life choices and considering a drastic change. The nosebleed that had created the pool of blood a few weeks earlier served as a wake-up call that my "extracurricular activities" were getting out of hand.

By January of 1985, I was enrolled at the University of Wisconsin–La Crosse, my once flowing mullet cut down to a more conventional length, the rock 'n' roll lifestyle squarely in the rearview mirror. I stopped doing drugs—at least those that aren't currently legal in a dozen or so U.S. states—and didn't play another note for over fifteen years.

Instead, I was wholly focused on my future with Linda, but even then I remained off-balance. I threw myself back into school—and later work—so heavily that I didn't have room for much else. For the next nine years, I regularly worked long hours, earning an undergraduate degree, then a Master's, and finally a Ph.D. Linda was the primary breadwinner during this period, but I held various positions to help out financially where I could.

By the time I reached my late thirties, I was successful in every conventional way, but I still wasn't happy. I was a father, business owner, and community leader, but it was all a façade. In hindsight, I now understand that even though I had gotten back onto the "right" path, I was still off-balance; I had swung too far.

Being off-balance almost assuredly results in hurting the people you care for most, because it renders you unable to open yourself up to other points of view. You become prone to making assumptions and taking people for granted. Being off-balance means, almost by definition, that you have a fixed mindset around certain aspects of your life. It causes you to become unyielding in certain circumstances, projecting your own lack of balance onto those around you, whether it's your direct reports, your family, or your community.

Everything started to unravel for me after two affairs caused me to eventually walk out on my family and file for divorce. I had this unshakable feeling that something was missing in my life and had foolishly convinced myself that another woman could fill the void. If you take nothing else away from my story, please know this: Wherever you are in life, I can assure you that the grass is never greener on the other side; it's just different grass. Noxious weeds will choke off and consume any lawn (relationship) if not properly fed and nurtured.

You can't go through life without ever hurting anybody, but that's not the point. "Life happens," but it takes a certain level of emotional intelligence, maturity, and self-awareness to recover. It's almost always the easier path to block out difficult and uncomfortable human emotions and take a more directive, my-way-or-the-highway approach to life. When someone calls you out on your mistakes, especially someone you take for granted, it can be very painful, and it takes real resilience and perspective to work through it and move on.

Harboring ill feelings might be easier than addressing them, but when left unaddressed, those feelings can calcify and manifest in other ways. Our instinct in life and in business is to take painful experiences and put them in a box where we don't have to look at them; that, to me, is no way to go through life. However, it took far too long for me to figure that out.

Although Linda and I were only apart for roughly eighteen months, it took a lot of hard work and soul searching to repair the damage I had caused and find our way back to each other. Fortunately, I was able to find a new kind of balance through the process of marriage counseling. It was very difficult work; don't let anyone tell you otherwise. Our first three counselors helped us a bit here and there, but it wasn't until we began working with the fourth that we were equipped with tools we could bring home and use to continue making progress on our own.

Only through counseling, and the love of my wife, was I able to achieve the balance I have today. Counseling allowed Linda and me to put our family back together, but this was not achievable without real pain, heartache, persistence, and perseverance.

Up until my early forties, I was very one-dimensional; first wholly focused on school, then wholly focused on becoming a rock star, then wholly focused on completing my education and starting a family, and eventually wholly focused on work. During this difficult period, I finally started singing again and poured music back into my life.

Through the course of my lifetime, rock 'n' roll has gone from a calling to a vice to eventually a wake-up call that I can (and should) do more than just be the leader of a business. If you're all about just one thing, you're likely setting yourself up for disaster, especially if that thing is work. Being an effective business leader requires balance, and that is something I have finally achieved after decades of having it all and still feeling like I had nothing. Through this book, I hope to help you achieve the same sense of balance.

PART 1

Leadership for the Next Generation

We're in the midst of a tectonic shift in what it means to be an effective leader. For most of my career, leaders were chosen because they demonstrated strong technical skills, were able to play and win at the game of workplace politics, or demonstrated supreme loyalty to the leaders and decision makers who came before them.

That generation of leaders was encouraged to rule with unflinching confidence, often from behind a closed door. They sought to demonstrate strength above all else and did so at the expense of the well-being of their subordinates.

Unapproachable, uncaring, and unbalanced leaders created an epidemic of disillusionment within the lower ranks of their organizations, one that we still haven't fully healed from today. Nobody begins their career wanting to be disillusioned and discouraged about their future. Most of us begin our careers full of enthusiasm, excitement, and potential; all it takes is one discouraging leader or experience to extinguish that fire.

In order to do their jobs effectively, I believe leaders need to demonstrate balance: balance between strength and vulnerability, confidence and self-lessness, passion and measure, single-mindedness and inclusivity, determination and curiosity, and leadership and followership.

Beyond the balance we should all strive for as individuals, in the world of work we also need to do a better job at balancing our technical abilities with our more human characteristics, with an eye toward building workplaces and a society that hold an appreciation for both. Fortunately, these two types of balance are interrelated. By becoming less robotic and more empathetic, emotionally intelligent, and communicative, we can achieve better outcomes in our personal *and* professional lives.

I've been striving toward achieving a greater balance in my life for almost two decades, and while I've made progress, there's always more work to be done. For example, I take pride in being calm, level headed, and analytical. I'm not the most approachable person you've met, but I'm working on it. I'm also working on being more open-minded and inclusive of other perspectives, cultures, and opinions.

Lately, I've taken a few steps backward on my personal continuous improvement journey and believe that, as a society, we're collectively taking steps backward. I find myself being quick to judge others and engaging in conversations I would have historically avoided. "Did you hear about so-and-so? I can't believe they _____. I never would have . . ."

This is not who I want to be.

I can't be a force for good in this world if I'm being "judgy." Being judgmental in a nonconstructive fashion doesn't fit with this goal. It may feel good in the moment to be the smartest guy in the room, even if it means belittling another person or team, but there is real and lasting fallout from those short-term "wins."

As an example of this lasting fallout, in the seventh grade I was in music class with a very dear friend of mine—we'll call her Billie to protect the innocent. One day in class, we were all practicing a song we were to perform at the next assembly. Billie was singing away at the top of her lungs with great enthusiasm when the teacher stopped the song midverse and told her to stand in the back and lip-synch for the performance. Billie complied but, as you can imagine, was devastated inside. She was a tough cookie and didn't show emotion, but she would never sing another note again outside of the shower. Sadly, Billie recently lost her battle with cancer. Before she passed, she would recount the story periodically with a grin, even though I could tell that deep down she was still hurt from the experience. That music teacher created a scar many years ago that never healed.

Before we move on, I need to step onto my soapbox for a moment to promote my passions for music and math. Back then, music was a mandatory class, which is a policy I agree with and wish we would go back to. Everyone should know how to count and understand basic musical structure. Math and music are inextricably linked, so understanding one helps with the other and vice versa. The world would be a better place if we made this connection more clear in our schools so as to grow our collective level of musical and mathematical literacy.

Contrary to learning the difference between a quarter note and a half note, developing the skill of singing can be quite variable due to the physical differences of our vocal chords, breath support systems, and ear/nasal structures. It's hard, but almost anyone can sing at some level of proficiency. Unfortunately, in our modern society, if you don't sing like a pop star, you're told you "can't sing" and are encouraged to stop.

You Are Responsible for Your Own Wake

I am a boater and have been plying the waters of the Upper Mississippi River since I was a boy. One of the most important lessons you learn as a boater is that you are responsible for your own wake. The wake you throw off depends on the size, weight, and speed of your vessel. The waves that your boat generates can damage the environment, destroy property, and cause personal injury. Therefore, as an experienced boater, you are constantly evaluating your surroundings and anticipating the impact your wake will have on other boaters and the shoreline.

On balance, boaters are a curiously courteous and helpful group of people. On the water, people wave at total strangers as if they're best friends, and they look out for one another when they find someone in distress. This makes sense when you realize that any body of water can turn from idyllic to treacherous in the blink of an eye. The wake your boat creates is an integral part of the ecosystem and can be quite damaging if not managed carefully.

One day we were enjoying a beautiful Sunday afternoon on the Mississippi with a few of our friends and family, including my wife's then 101-year-old grandmother. Our boat is classified as a cruiser, which is basically a motorhome that floats. As we were putting along, another large vessel approached from our stern at full speed, and it was throwing off a huge wake. It passed me with just seventy-five feet of clearance on our starboard side, leaving me no time to course correct or prepare for the impact of its wake. Our boat rocked violently, sending appetizers—and grandmother—flying. Fortunately, no one was injured, and no damage was caused, but it could have been much worse. If it had been, both the pilot and the owner of the other boat would have been directly accountable for any damage that occurred.

A boat's wake is a temporary but potentially powerful reminder of its presence on the water. The bigger the boat, the greater the level of responsibility that the captain bears.

Here's the point: Leaders at all levels leave a wake as they interact with the organization—the higher up you are in the company, the bigger the wake you throw off. It's your responsibility to be aware of your wake and the impact it could have on individuals and teams, both within your immediate surroundings as well as further downstream.

Most experienced leaders will immediately connect with the point of this parable. If you're an experienced leader, I'm sure you can recall times where something you did or said inadvertently had a lasting negative impact on a team or team member. You likely learned from that experience and vowed to improve your level of awareness of the impact you have on others.

However, there are those senior managers whose egos and lack of behavioral training limit their ability to understand how their wake impacts their surroundings. These managers likely reached their level in the organization based on technical expertise but never invested themselves in grooming their emotional intelligence skill set.

The best managers continually optimize the balance between their technical and behavioral skills. They have a keen understanding of their surroundings and the impact they can have on others. High-performing leaders also carefully balance their views as they look into the future by ensuring that previous decisions and interactions have not had unintended negative consequences on their environment.

Teach, Coach, Mentor, and Inspire (TCMI)[1]

Now think of your role as a manager or an influencer in a business. You are responsible for a team and are in a position of authority. If a simple interaction between a music teacher and a student can cut so deep that its effect lasts a lifetime, imagine the impact a few carelessly uttered words can have on your colleagues. Whether you like it or not, your voice is loud and leaves a powerful wake. As you speak, those around you will pick your words apart for context and subtext.

Some of your key roles are to teach, coach, mentor, and inspire. Others are to assess talent and provide constructive feedback to your team members so that one day they can surpass you. As an influencer, you walk a fine line. You need to find a balance that allows you to judge without being judgmental—to criticize constructively. Sometimes you need to take control of a situation and be the smartest person in the room. It's much harder—but equally rewarding—to help others develop and grow by allowing them to shine.

To minimize the risk of inadvertently hurting your work partners with your words, it's important to provide them with regular and consistent coaching and feedback. Unfortunately, those who have put little effort into developing skills like emotional intelligence and effective communication will likely struggle with this quintessential managerial function.

Challenging conversations are called "challenging conversations" for a reason. A feedback session can be difficult for both the sender and the receiver. To make them less challenging, *make the time* to provide coaching and feedback more often. If you're waiting for the annual performance review to provide feedback, anxiety will build on both sides. The sender will do a less-than-effective job of providing feedback, and the receiver will likely be so nervous that they hear very little of what's being said.

---

1. We love acronyms at Kaplan—I just made this one up!

When you provide feedback more often, the receiver will digest it more readily, and you'll do a better job as a sender because it will feel more natural to do so.

My dear wife, Linda, is a horse person. I'm not. When I get nervous around these graceful animals, they can sense it and will either take advantage of my anxiety or get anxious too and spin out of control. The same thing happens in human interactions. If you're well-balanced, objective, and data driven, a coaching/feedback session is likely to go much better for both parties.

It's incumbent on leaders to create such opportunities for personal and professional development. Nothing says "I care" more than helping another human develop and grow. If you create learning opportunities for your team, both formal and informal, it will pay dividends for both individual and team performance for years to come. Speak the truth in your constructive criticism and follow it up with action to help the recipient get better.

We live in a dangerous time of "always on" communication and entertainment. There is a cacophony of voices all competing with one another for eyeballs and ears—trying to outdo themselves with ever more salacious details of political intrigue and celebrity gossip. Ubiquitous access to social media has turned us all into pundits of the everyday goings-on of our friends and neighbors. Civility and humility in our society are wilting away, replaced by partisanship and self-importance. We're becoming more unbalanced. We have more opportunities than ever to let slip that life-changing negative commentary just so we can get the high of feeling important in the moment.

None of us is perfect, but we all need to do better—myself included. I try to rebalance myself by thinking more overtly about the power of the wake my words can leave behind, and I try my best to use my words for good.

The Light in Your Eyes

When I'm interviewing job candidates, one of the primary things I'm looking for is that intangible "X factor"; a certain light in the candidate's eyes that shows their motivation and ability to learn and grow.

I subscribe to the old adage that the eyes are the window to the soul. By using the eyes (as well as reading other body language), I find I can get a good read on whether the candidate is genuinely interested in speaking with me. The eyes tell a story of confidence (or lack thereof) and frequently give the candidate away if they're not interested in performing certain aspects of the job. The candidate's words may be saying one thing, but if the eyes aren't tracking with what's being said, then there may be challenges ahead.

During my daily routine with colleagues and team members, I look for this "light" and try to note its consistency across interactions. Emerging leaders with the potential to grow one or two levels beyond their current role typically show their light consistently across myriad situations and pressure levels. From my perspective, this is a clear signal that the individual can handle more. If there's one place that stress and pressure show up, it's in the eyes. When people tell you "it's written all over your face," that's what they mean.

Let's discuss a specific example. James (yes, that's his real name) joined our company as a fresh-faced university graduate in sales. When we interviewed him, we knew he had something special—he possessed the raw technical skill needed to perform the job, was a great cultural fit (values and behaviors), and had the light in his eyes. There was a lot more in the tank—he had the willingness and ability to take on more with the right guidance and development. In short order, James was proving us right and was excelling at his work, bringing new perspectives and opportunities to the business.

More than a decade later, James is still with the business and continues to grow. The light remains in his eyes, and we are still confident that there's more in the tank. Why? Because he had the light to start with and was paired with a solid manager who spent the time to work on James's development and growth.

This story could have turned out much differently had James been paired with a bad manager, one who didn't understand the power and weight of their voice. If he had been paired with a poor manager, James would have likely quit years ago, leading to recruitment and lost productivity costs, as well as the loss of a shining light from the business. Unfortunately, I've seen this happen far too often and have been slow at times to make this connection to explain the departure. A poor manager will place blame for the loss at the feet of the employee, saying things like "she was a poor fit" or "he was problematic to manage." Both statements are typically hiding the root cause—that the loss was really the result of the manager's unwillingness or inability to invest in and develop the light that shone so brightly at the outset of the employment relationship.

While poor leadership can quickly extinguish the light in a high-potential hire's eyes, providing a supportive working environment can help nurture the light and keep it shining brighter as time goes on. When you find an organization that offers that kind of supportive, nurturing, and balanced environment, leaving it becomes very difficult.

Opportunity, Joy, and Purpose at Work

On November 22, 1999, Linda and I signed the final documents to sell Temte's Financial Education to Kaplan. Temte's Financial was an affiliate of the Schweser Study Program for the CFA Exam. We sold video lessons that were designed to complement the venerable Schweser Study Notes.

You never forget the day you sell your business. At the time of the sale, I thought I would spend a few years getting the business on an even keel within the Kaplan portfolio and then go off and try something new. The entrepreneurial bug had bitten me quite hard, so it seemed logical that I would explore other options after things were stable.

During the first few years of my tenure, the business grew like a weed. Within a three-year span, revenue and operating income doubled, and we launched the first digital Qbank product in the history of CFA review, as well as Kaplan's first video-based live online program. Needless to say, we were rock'n and roll'n. The Kaplan culture promoted this kind of innovation, and the autonomy we were given to transform the business was extraordinary.

Time flew by as we globalized and launched new products—leapfrogging our competition and cementing our place as the dominant force in the advanced financial designations marketplace. Before I knew it, I was celebrating my tenth anniversary and had been named president of Kaplan Professional, assuming responsibility for a much broader product portfolio.

Kaplan's values are Integrity, Knowledge, Support, Opportunity, and Results. Each of these words resonates with me, but it was clear after year ten that if I continued to apply myself, I would find even more opportunity within the Kaplan family. Over the next five years, in addition to my Kaplan Professional duties, I served as the president of Kaplan University's (now Purdue Global) College of Business and Technology, which allowed me to further hone and explore my academic leadership capabilities. I also served as president of a small college in New Hampshire, which we attempted to move from a traditional classroom-based model to a fully online, adult workforce development program. Opportunity was all around me. Our team learned with each "failure," and successes were celebrated.

Early in my career at Kaplan, I came to understand that joy and purpose were built into the fabric of the company, which is what made it such a desirable place to work. After all, at our core, we're educators—one of the noble professions in society.

I recall vividly the employee town hall where I uttered the following words during a rough patch in the company's history. The team was navigating through significant change, and team members were understandably uncertain about their roles and their futures at the company. I said, "Today, I got into my car and drove to work like I do every day. It struck me that I was not on my way to work but was, instead, on my way to a place where I'm able to help individuals achieve their educational and career goals."

I remain at Kaplan more than twenty-one years after the sale of my business because no matter how tough the sledding or difficult the challenge, I am able to remind myself of that town hall and the looks on team members' faces as they too realized that purpose and joy were built into our DNA.

Unfortunately, I see many people in our society who expect that opportunity will be magically bestowed upon them. They've grown up in coddled, "everyone gets a prize" schools and homes. They believe the business world owes them something for just showing up. Here's my message for the younger generations who are in college or starting their careers: Opportunity comes to those who are continuously learning, moving forward, and applying their talents in a constructive fashion. If one sits back and waits for an opportunity to knock, the wait will be long and frustrating. The ego must be balanced, because over the long term, opportunity aligns itself with authenticity.

A Night at the Theater

In December of 2019, Linda and I combined some business with pleasure in the Big Apple. We like taking in Broadway theater productions and enjoy exploring the diverse restaurants in the city.

Prior to seeing *Moulin Rouge* (recommended for those who love dance and pop), we went to a restaurant we've frequented on several occasions. We've had good experiences there in the past. We like it because there's good beer, good food, and friendly staff; most important, they're efficient. When theater is involved, getting to our seats on time is the top priority.

On this particular night, we entered the restaurant and immediately noticed something was amiss. The host, we'll call her "Jenny," was standing behind the welcome station angrily punching the touchscreen on her computer monitor—swearing like a sailor. We stood there for a few minutes, bemused at the scene. When she finally looked up, she glanced our way, made eye contact, and stormed off.

After a minute or so, another staff member walked past, asked if we had been helped, and promptly found us a table. As we ordered our drinks and dinner, we watched Jenny with interest. She was berating servers, ignoring customers, and continuing to use profanity as she interacted with her computer.

Our initial impression was that Jenny was just having a bad day. As the evening progressed, though, it became clear that tonight's performance was closer to the norm than the exception. Coworkers ignored her, and we overheard other team members talking about how uncomfortable they felt around her.

Jenny wasn't having a bad day; Jenny was *actively disengaged*. She didn't like her work, her coworkers, or her customers.

The annual employee engagement survey has become part of the fabric of most corporations. Chances are you've completed some type of survey that asks an array of questions to probe how you like the company you work for, the effectiveness of your manager, the culture, and the work you do each day.

There's usually a burst of activity around the collation, interpretation, and dissemination of results. Results are usually grouped into three or four categories: fully engaged, partially engaged, indifferent, and disengaged (or similar). Team meetings are held and action plans are established, with the aim to make your company a "Great Place to Work." Those plans, or "Great Place" initiatives, address the most high-yield categories of identified organizational challenges, and managers are charged with executing those plans.

In the best companies, those action plans are given priority, resources, and focus throughout the year. Typically, action plans are pointed at influencing those who have expressed partial engagement or indifference. This is the "moveable middle" in your organization—employees who are not completely engaged but have the potential to become more engaged if given focus and attention. To be cold and calculating, the moveable middle has the highest potential return on investment (ROI) from intervention.

While the moveable middle gets most of the attention, we also can't ignore the actively disengaged. This category doesn't get much attention, because it's represented visually as the "thin red line" at the bottom of the bar chart that shows employees lumped into the aforementioned categories. The ROI from intervention is low, and the number of data points appears to be inconsequential. Actively disengaged team members, however, represent a real risk to their employers. The story of Jenny should be a cautionary tale for business leaders at all levels.

Although Linda and I used the restaurant experience as an opportunity to observe and learn, we were simultaneously appalled at the behavior we witnessed. Most importantly, we have to assume there was a manager on staff that evening who allowed the behavior to continue. The manager was allowing the business's reputation to be damaged. The manager was allowing Jenny to drag down her coworkers. Studies show that there are a lot of Jennys out there. While modern management practices are helping to close the gap, few organizations don't suffer from the effects of having disengaged employees.

When Gallup began tracking employee engagement rates in the United States in the year 2000, it found that only 26 percent of Americans were engaged in their work, which it defined as "those who are involved in, enthusiastic about and committed to their work and workplace."[2] Perhaps even more concerning, 18 percent were actively disengaged, which Gallup defined as "workers who have miserable work experiences." When Gallup expanded its scope in 2016, it identified a "worldwide employee engagement crisis" after finding that only 13 percent of employees around the globe were engaged in their work.[3]

Much about how we work has changed since then, and engagement continues to trend upward. However, there's still a long way to go. In July of 2020, Gallup reported[4] that a record high 40 percent of Americans were engaged in their work, and a record low of 13 percent were actively disengaged. The remaining 47 percent were still "not engaged," which the organization defined as "psychologically unattached to their work and company," adding that "they're also on the lookout for better employment opportunities and will quickly leave their company for a slightly better offer." In other words, these employees represent the "moveable middle."

Each disengaged employee costs the employer roughly 34 percent of the employee's annual salary, according to Gallup. Said differently, 34 percent of what the company spends to employ that individual goes to waste. That's because each disengaged employee has 37 percent higher absenteeism, 18 percent lower productivity, and 15 percent lower profitability. Perhaps most significant, the research firm found that managers account

2. *Employee Engagement on the Rise in the U.S.*, August 26, 2018, Jim Harter; Gallup.
3. *The Worldwide Employee Engagement Crisis*, January 7, 2016, Annamarie Mann & Jim Harter; Gallup.
4. *U.S. Employee Engagement Hits New High After Historic Drop*, July 22, 2020, Jim Harter; Gallup.

for at least 70 percent of the variance in team engagement.[5] There's an old adage that says people don't leave their company, they leave their manager. Now there's plenty of research to back it up.

Middle managers have a vital role to play in creating an engaged, loyal, and productive workforce, but all too often these leaders are ill-equipped to do so. They were trained in institutions that emphasize the importance of mastering technical skills, without nurturing their ability to master human skills like empathy, communication, and emotional intelligence. I'll be the first to admit that for much of my career I thought these traits were secondary, if important at all, but years of experience have caused me to change my tune.

Without addressing the actively disengaged, people like Jenny will continue to slip through the cracks and damage their employer's reputation. After that experience, Linda and I were certain we would not go back to that particular restaurant, even though it was once a favorite. With the high and rising cost of new customer acquisition across industries, our negative experience represents a real loss for the business. It's unlikely we're the only ones who had this perception and made the same decision.

Whether you recognize it or not, it's highly likely that you have a Jenny on your team or somewhere within your orbit. Unlike the indifferent or moveable middle, Jenny is poisoning your team. Jenny doesn't care about the quality of her work or the outcomes experienced by your customers. Worse yet, Jenny may actually be trying to subvert the performance of the team and intentionally damage your business's reputation.

Sometimes it's blindingly obvious, as in the case of Jenny. Even when it's obvious to others, as a leader or manager, you might be blind to the Jennys under your watch. Jenny likely started her job with a light in her eyes. She interviewed well and came into the job with glowing references.

---

5. *Dismal Employee Engagement Is a Sign of Global Mismanagement*, 2017, Jim Harter; Gallup.

Our egos routinely get in the way of our identifying the actively disengaged. In addition to our built-in wiring to look for the positive in human interaction, it's very difficult for us to admit failure and genuinely take on board the feedback of others. "How could Jenny possibly be actively disengaged? I was the hiring manager and have a great track record of hiring productive team members who fit with the culture! How dare my peers challenge Jenny's performance!"

What Can We Do?

So how can we improve organizational performance by identifying the actively disengaged and helping them discover other opportunities elsewhere (one door closes, another opens)?

Managers can start by looking carefully for the light in their employees' eyes. Nurture their light by challenging them and providing the right development opportunities at the right time. Remember, at the top of the list of your standard work is to teach, coach, mentor, and inspire.

Treat the performance review process with the respect it deserves. The key is documentation. Linda would harp on me when we worked together, and her voice still rings in my ears around the office: "Documentation, documentation, documentation." If you don't document performance conversations, as well as the challenges your version of Jenny is creating for the organization, performance data won't support the actions that need to be taken. Moving her on to greener pastures will be more difficult and costly than it needs to be.

Listen to your peers. When we receive feedback on our direct reports, our instinct is to recoil and not believe the information being presented. We feel resentful and minimize the feedback, or we ignore it altogether. Worse yet, we dig in our heels and convince ourselves that we're going to "teach Jim a lesson"—that it's his problem, not ours. Open ears and an open mind should be the modus operandi.

It's also important to listen to your customers. Too often, we're not drilling into our qualitative Net Promoter Score (NPS) feedback or direct customer survey responses. I can't tell you how many times I've left constructively critical feedback on the performance of a company's representative or agent only to hear crickets from the other side. If you're asking customers to tell you how you're doing, listen and respond.

Stay connected to your people, and be aware of any changes in their behavior or mood. These could be early signs that something is impacting energy or motivation levels. This is where your emotional intelligence can really pay off by getting an early read on a challenge with a coworker, an assignment that's pushing the employee too far, or a situation outside of the office that's affecting performance. You can't be a mind reader, but if you're astute and empathetic, you may be able to rectify a situation before it calcifies and becomes intractable.

Most important, don't let your ego get in the way. One of the hardest, but most mission-critical, things you do as a manager is to hire people who complement your skills and help push the team to new heights. Be confident in your own abilities and take it as a mark of honor if one of your "shining lights" eventually outshines you. In organizationally healthy companies, this will be viewed as a positive, not a negative.

As I write this, I'm reminiscing back to missed "people development" opportunities during my career, particularly the times when I lost track of the light in a top performer's eyes. My ego has definitely gotten in the way, and I've missed important opportunities for employee development and growth that could have helped to ensure long-term success for both the business and the employee. My job is to teach, coach, mentor, and inspire—to ensure that the light shines brightly in our teams.

Whether you recognize it or not, disengaged team members are crying out for your help. It's likely they took the job you offered and haven't really connected with the business, culture, or customers. They may have gone through a life change and have reevaluated who they want to be, and the current job doesn't match with those revised expectations. Maybe they oversold themselves and their skill level. Maybe they had a run-in with other team members and have decided to make things difficult for everyone else to right a wrong. It's likely they feel stuck and don't know what to do. Sometimes, as a leader you need to show people kindness and help them see what's possible by forcing a change to the status quo.

Remember, in business you are what you measure, and you are what you allow. It's this last bit that we often forget. Think back in your career to individuals or teams that were disengaged or misconfigured. Did you look the other way? Did you ignore feedback from peers? Did your ego get in the way? Allowing Jenny to continue in her role could damage your reputation and will certainly cost the company time and money. Real money.

Oh, if you self-identify as Jenny, do everyone a favor (including yourself). Be brave. Self-select out. Move on with dignity.

Disorder, Chaos, and Growth

Businesses are powered by humans. When a business is created, it is typically formed by a sole proprietor or a small team, and an essential initial condition is a deep sense of trust within the nucleus of the entity. The success or failure of the venture depends on it.

While not always the case, a key goal for most businesses is growth and profitability. As the business grows, teams expand, and the level of intimacy among team members begins to erode. Walls are erected between teams to protect a sense of team identity. This happens because there is an upper limit to managerial effectiveness in a nuclear team.[6]

---

6. *Is Your Team Too Big? Too Small? What's the Right Number?* June 16, 2006; Wharton School of Business.

When team size increases, cliques begin to form as like-minded individuals begin to coalesce. As the business grows, more nuclear teams are established as more specialization is needed to achieve scale. The concept of "us versus them" takes hold, and competition is established *within* the business. A critical mass is reached where trust among teams is no longer the initial assumption. Mistrust becomes pervasive as teams compete for resources and team goals begin to diverge from overarching corporate goals.

If you've worked in an academic or a business setting for any length of time, you have witnessed this behavior firsthand. Individual opinions begin to influence team dynamics, and an "anchor dragger" can pull down an entire team or turn teams against one another.

As a new manager, entrepreneur, or seasoned leader, it's important to understand the dynamics of team size as the business grows. Unfortunately, this subject gets very little airtime in business school—my hypothesis is that team size dynamics[7] are a leading cause of business and project failure, yet we tend to focus precious little energy on addressing the problem (more on that in part 2).

I won't get into the physical definition of entropy,[8] but it's a word we should all know. Loosely speaking, entropy is defined as the natural tendency for a system to disintegrate or fall apart. The more complex the system is, the more opportunities for disorder and chaos to be found within it. When applied to business, the larger and more complex the company, the more opportunity there is for disagreement and misalignment among teams and team members.

---

7. This hypothesis is supported by a handful of academic studies but needs much more investigation. Examples include *The Effect of Team Size on Management Team Performance: The Mediating Role of Relationship Conflict and Team Cohesion*, by Lars Erik Espedalen, 2016; Psykologisk Institutt and *Group Size, Group Development, and Group Productivity*, by Susan A. Wheelan, 2009; SAGE Publications.

8. Entropy is a measure of the degree of disorder in a substance or a system: entropy always increases and available energy diminishes in a closed system, according to Dictionary.com.

Entropy as a natural state is why investing in organizational health is so important in all business settings. Marriages take work to maintain and flourish, friendships take work to have any kind of permanence—why don't we think the same way in business?

If you've been through any kind of marriage or relationship counseling, you are acutely aware that building and maintaining communication skills is the key to the relationship's longevity. Developing the ability to deliver and accept constructive criticism, to both challenge and actively listen to other points of view, and to do so in a respectful and civil manner are all skills that need constant attention. These skills translate directly into a business setting.

I can personally attest that in a previous version of myself as a leader, I believed communication skills were just "fluff" and made them a low priority for investment. By applying the lessons learned through my own marriage counseling journey, I've learned that ensuring team members are equipped with the ability to engage in frank and fearless conversations is a necessary ingredient in building the trust that's essential for healthy teams. This is why communication skills are typically listed as a top priority in solving the skills gap—effective communication is vital in all organizations and becomes increasingly important as complexity increases.

I strongly recommend adding "Fight Entropy" to your list of standard work[9] and placing it toward the top of the list. When you create clear goals for your teams and ensure that these goals are congruent with overarching corporate objectives, the likelihood of conflict and chaos is reduced. In fact, the conditions for trust to flourish are reestablished—much like when the business was in its infancy. In this environment, teams and

---

9. Standard work is simply the list of steps for a process that is the most efficient path to desired outcomes. Standard work is then continually refined to remove waste, enhance teamwork, and improve performance (with a maniacal focus on the customer). We will discuss leader standard work in greater detail in part 6.

individuals see how their work contributes to customer satisfaction and business success—leading to more situations where everyone is rowing at the same cadence and in the same direction.

During my junior year of college, I took a math logic course as part of my computer science minor. The primary thing I learned from that experience was that the best logical proofs are almost always simple and elegant. Early in the course, I would find myself turning in homework with proofs that contained more steps than necessary—the instructor would invariably come back and present the class with a three- or four-line answer. I don't mean to geek out on you here, but the point is that simplification, parsimony, and elegance won the day.

The same concept holds in business. Unnecessary complexity is one of the most insidious forms of waste. Complexity drives up costs, reduces flexibility, and ultimately harms the consumer experience.

Ironically, some of your employees like unnecessary complexity—they use it as a security blanket to prevent others from understanding how work flows from point A to point B. They rationalize it this way, "Better to live with a little chaos and inefficiency than risk losing one's job."

Worse yet, the protection of complex environments is typically not overt but, instead, lives in the subconscious. Many parts of the job—as currently defined—are wired into the subconscious brain, just as your trip to and from the office is. This is a primary "why" behind the length of time it takes to drive complexity out of systems—especially for established businesses populated by long-tenured team members.

When faced with this resistance to change, your role as a leader is to use change management tools and learning resources to help team members see the benefits of change and how a new set of standard work can help them grow both personally and professionally. Fighting entropy is a necessary, but not sufficient, condition for meeting business goals. There are many other key ingredients, like agility, innovation, balance, and differentiation, but I believe that if we all learn that regression to disorder is a natural process and to fight entropy earlier in the life cycle of the company as it grows, we will see more high-functioning teams, fewer artificial silos, improved trust, and ultimately, better business performance.

Creating balance is no easy task. It takes conscious effort and self-reflection to understand our own weaknesses, and it takes even more to correct our imbalances. However, I believe that you can't be an effective leader without going through that difficult but necessary process of self-assessment and course correction.

Exceptional leaders understand the power of their words, identify and nurture human potential, model organizational purpose, and adopt a continuous improvement mindset to minimize organizational entropy. We will be exploring these concepts in greater detail throughout the remainder of this book.

PART 2

Education and Lifelong Learning

In the early 1970s, my sisters and I would come home from school each afternoon and park ourselves in front of a cathode-ray tube, each with a gigantic bowl of ice cream. One of our favorite shows was *Star Trek*. For an hour each weekday, we imagined ourselves on the NCC-1701 cruising the galaxy with Mr. Spock and Captain Kirk—going where no one had gone before.

Star Trek made an indelible imprint on me in those formative years. I would frequently dream of being part of the crew, doing good deeds and learning something new in every port of call. The morality plays that were the subtext of each episode were not obvious to me at the time but have stuck with me as an adult.

As a child, our home planet seemed impossibly big—a green space to play in and explore with unlimited resources and potential. My love of *Star Trek* gave me a frame within which to fit the universe—which was even more mysterious and incomprehensibly vast. Through those afternoon adventures, I didn't feel so small and alone.

As an adult with "extensive experience," it is clear to me that our world isn't as large and limitless as I once imagined. Education and a global perspective have taught me that we all live on a spaceship that circles a large ball of plasma in an unremarkable corner of an unremarkable galaxy.[1]

To illustrate this, close your eyes and join me on a journey to view Earth from one million miles away. We hit the positioning thrusters and turn the spacecraft back toward home. Through the window, we see a large, rocky ball with white clouds and vast blue oceans as well as a smaller rocky ball in a tidally locked orbit circling around it (our moon).

If you consider this stunning picture, you quickly realize that everyone and everything we've ever known, touched, and felt is back on that rocky blue ball. At one million miles, our home still looks rather large and hospitable. Now imagine our spacecraft is *ten million* miles away.[2] At this vantage point, Earth is, as Carl Sagan famously called it, a "pale blue dot"[3] in a sea of pitch black. Here, it becomes obvious how small, insignificant, and fragile our place is in the universe.

I'm speaking like I've actually made this trip. Through my imaginary voyages on the starship *Enterprise* and with the help of NASA's real-life fleet of spacecraft (*Voyager 1, Voyager 2, Galileo*, etc.), I can paint an awesome image in my mind. From this viewpoint, our resources are clearly limited, and we're all on Spaceship Earth together.

Just seventy years ago, talking like this would have been edgy science fiction. Seven hundred years ago, I would have been burned at the stake. Seven thousand years ago, we were looking up to the sky with wonder and awe, just trying to make sense of it all. Today, with the right resources

---

1. Paraphrasing Stephen Hawking's famous quote from his 2010 book *The Grand Design*, published by Bantam Books.
2. For perspective, Mars is a little less than fifty million miles away from Earth (on average).
3. *Pale Blue Dot: A Vision of the Human Future in Space* by Carl Sagan was published in 1997 by Ballantine Books.

and technology, such a voyage is in the realm of feasibility. A mere five thousand years since the beginning of recorded history, we all have access to the knowledge necessary to dream realistically of our twenty-million mile round trip.

So, what's the point?

I'm thrilled you're still with me on our hypothetical journey. After we stick the landing back on Earth, we exit our spacecraft with a newfound sense of urgency to take care of our planet and each other, to use all the tools at our disposal to build a better world. The challenge appears so daunting and insurmountable that we ask ourselves where we should start. We're committed to making Spaceship Earth a better place for current and future generations, but how?

The answer is education.

Throughout history, education has played the role of the "great leveler." Social structures and societies have been transformed through education. We have clear examples that when education and creativity are stifled or reserved for the elite, our progress as a species is limited. When educational access is limited, entire swaths of the population are left behind or suppressed by those who are allowed into the club; our perspectives become more localized and narrow. We fight among ourselves for the betterment of a particular town, village, region, or country but almost always to the detriment of the planet as a whole.

With a limited education and a local-only view, it's easy to convince ourselves that resources are unlimited and that we should borrow from future generations to maximize current consumption and comfort in the world that immediately surrounds us.

Then again, my ice cream bowl is empty, the "red shirts" in the *Star Trek* landing party have all met an untimely demise, Kirk and Spock are back safely on the ship, and *Gilligan's Island* is on next.

Think Globally, Act Locally

At age twenty-one, as I was letting go of my dream to become a rock star, I fell madly in love with my soul mate and made a beeline for the University of Wisconsin–La Crosse to make the most important investment a person can make—pursuing an education. After testing the waters in the history department and settling on an economics degree, I quickly moved into finance for my graduate studies at the University of Iowa.

I really enjoyed the technical aspects of economics and finance. Most problems had answers, but there were typically a few ways to arrive at a solution; the lack of absolutes and black-and-white answers appealed to me. My critical-thinking skills were really getting a workout. My role as a teaching assistant allowed me to fine-tune my performance skills in the classroom (which would prove essential to the early success of the business Linda and I would later build with the Schwesers).

However, I was able to engineer the experience to nearly completely avoid behavioral training (a.k.a., soft skills). There was a department called Management and Organizations down the hall, and I avoided it like the plague. My thinking was that the mumbo jumbo they were working on would not apply to me in the career journey I was on. Oh, and forget about the marketing department—who needs sales and marketing? Looking back through the lens of time, I realize that both perspectives were huge misses for me. The majority of my work life over the last thirty years has been managing teams and selling: selling myself, selling my team's ideas, and selling the products we created!

Back in the late 1980s and early 1990s, the business world had not yet grasped the value of healthy teams. Patrick Lencioni's *The Five Dysfunctions of a Team*[4] wouldn't be published until 2002. By now it's become crystal clear that organizations that embark on continuous improvement and organizational health journeys are more sustainable and outperform rivals who do not do this work. A 2014 McKinsey study found that healthy companies generated shareholder returns that were three times higher than those of unhealthy companies.[5]

The employees who populate every organization today are the product of an educational system with two primary objectives: to create great citizens of the world and to create job-ready graduates. A tremendous amount of debate occurs in academic circles surrounding the roles and responsibilities of various educational entities in achieving these two primary objectives. For now, let's set those arguments aside. Instead, let's simply state that to do better than we are today will take commitment from mentors, parents, educational institutions, governments, and corporations to prioritize and democratize learning while simultaneously improving cost and access. Healthy tension should exist among these groups to promote creativity and test new perspectives.

Historically, almost all educational opportunities were local, with curriculum designed by those who held power. The definition of a "well-rounded" education varied widely and fit with the needs of regional leaders who needed to align the skills of the citizenry with the economic and political demands of the time.

As our world gets ever smaller through increasing digital interconnectedness and becomes more complex as humans work with and alongside machines of ever-greater capability, we must instill new competencies into the workforce of the future. Don't just take my word

---

4. Published April 11, 2002; Jossey-Bass.
5. *McKinsey Quarterly*, April 2014, "The Hidden Value of Organizational Health and How to Capture It," by Aaron De Smet, Bill Schaninger, and Matthew Smith.

for it. That sentiment is also shared by the World Economic Forum,[6] UNESCO,[7] the OECD,[8] the Brookings Institution,[9] the Pew Research Center,[10] the *Harvard Business Review*,[11] and plenty of other equally reputable institutions.

Having technical intelligence will not be enough for us to survive and thrive in the world of tomorrow. Emotional intelligence will be of equal, if not greater, importance to ensure we maintain positive relationships with each other and with the planet.[12] The ability of the average human to engage in constructive, multipronged dialogue, to understand varying points of view, to empathize with people who look and behave differently than themselves, and to reach mutually beneficial compromises will be essential to our survival as a species.

Hence, educators of all varieties should be working to promote the development of enhanced emotional quotients (EQs).[13] That is why the World Economic Forum ranked a variety of human skills—such as emotional intelligence, leadership and social influence, creativity, and critical thinking—among the top ten emerging skills for the next decade.[14]

For the foreseeable future, Spaceship Earth is our only viable home. In both our personal and professional capacities, we need to treat her and

---

6. *Towards a Reskilling Revolution*, the World Economic Forum in collaboration with Boston Consulting Group, January 2019.
7. *The Futures of Learning 1: Why must learning content and methods change in the 21st century?* Cynthia Luna Scott, 2015; UNESCO.
8. *The Future of Education and Skills*, 2018; OECD.
9. *Why we need to rethink education in the artificial intelligence age*, January 31, 2019, John R. Allen; https://www.brookings.edu
10. *The Future of Jobs and Jobs Training*, May 3, 2017, Lee Rainie and Janna Anderson; https://www.pewresearch.org
11. *To Prepare for Automation, Stay Curious and Don't Stop Learning*, October 8, 2019, Tiger Tyagarajan, https://hbr.org
12. Think of Emotional Intelligence as the ability to effectively interpret the interplay between self, place, and others to determine appropriate situational responses.
13. The Cambridge Dictionary describes EQ as "a measurement of a person's emotional intelligence, [or] their ability to understand their own feelings and the feelings of others."
14. *Towards a Reskilling Revolution*, the World Economic Forum in collaboration with Boston Consulting Group, January 2019.

her inhabitants with respect and dignity. Any other approach is simply kicking the can down the road to future generations and exacerbating our current real and acute challenges.

If I could hop into a time machine and have a coaching session with my early mentors, I'd ask them to stress to Young Andy the behavioral aspect of business and the importance of the softer, human skills.

The Reskilling Revolution Versus the Clay Layer

That world of science fiction that once captured my imagination is getting closer to reality as a result of a number of technological leaps in recent years. Today, artificial intelligence is no longer a futuristic fantasy, and as it becomes a greater part of our daily lives, the need for a new approach toward education becomes even more pronounced. New technologies are quickly rendering existing roles obsolete and creating new roles that didn't exist previously, requiring individuals and organizations to readily adapt to a new and quickly evolving labor market. This next great leap is putting a greater emphasis on skills that many, including myself, long wrote off as secondary or as someone else's responsibility.

In January of 2019, the World Economic Forum laid out a compelling case for a "Reskilling Revolution" to respond to the needs of the future job market. It found that 60 percent of corporations consider a skills gap in their local market to be the primary barrier to adopting new technologies. These technologies include artificial intelligence (AI), data analytics, machine learning, and the Internet of things (IoT)—the very technologies that corporations will need to compete today and into the future. Perhaps even more concerning, 46 percent cited a lack of leadership capability as the primary barrier to adoption.[15]

---

15. *Towards a Reskilling Revolution*, the World Economic Forum in collaboration with Boston Consulting Group, January 2019.

The professional job clusters that will experience the most disruption in the coming decade, according to a follow-up report by the World Economic Forum published in January of 2020, are not exclusive to technology roles. These clusters include positions ranging from sales and marketing to human resources and management.[16]

To utilize the new technologies that are becoming a competitive necessity in most roles and industries—and to survive and thrive in an economy that will be defined by technological disruption—we will have to reform our approach to education. Meeting the challenge of the Reskilling Revolution will depend on having a mentally agile workforce that is able to change as the demand-side characteristics for labor rapidly evolve. Lifelong learning—that is, the continuous development of individual skills and capabilities—will soon be a baseline condition for labor-market participation.

Unfortunately, that requirement comes in direct opposition to the learning model that we've all become accustomed to. Most professionals view their learning days as long behind them. The Reskilling Revolution is on a crash course with a society that is not prepared to go back to school.

This tension is most visible within the "clay layer" or "permafrost" that exists within every organization. Both terms refer to the set of middle managers and individual contributors who have become disengaged and disillusioned regarding their career prospects and subconsciously (in some cases, consciously) resist change. Instead of taking a "we can" or "let's get going" stance when confronted with change, this group digs in their heels and says, "If we resist long enough, this too shall pass."

Resistance to change is a natural tendency that stems from a fear of loss of control—or in this case, employment—and a desire for consistency. The

---

16. *Jobs of Tomorrow*, The World Economic Forum, January 2020, page 13.

need for security and safety ranks just above the need for food, water, and shelter in Maslow's hierarchy.[17]

Without buy-in from middle management, however, there will be nobody to identify and nurture the vast trove of potential that lies within and beneath the clay layer. Middle managers are, after all, the gatekeepers of the organization's next generation of talent.

If disengaged middle managers are unable or unwilling to identify those who could potentially meet or exceed their own skill and talent level in the future, the best and brightest won't get the recognition or opportunity they deserve. Without recognition and opportunity, those high-potential team members will eventually begin to feel disengaged and disillusioned about their own career prospects. The light in their eyes will begin to fade.

Both change and learning rely on consciously wading into uncharted territory and being purposefully uncomfortable. Hence, doing the hard work of adopting a lifelong learning attitude and being both agile and accepting of change run counter to our human nature.

We live in a world where many are so comforted by the knowledge they already have—because it makes their world simple and understandable—that they resist any information that might challenge their worldview. For example, if you've determined, based on your education and life experiences, that the Earth is flat, the learning process required to get you to a place where you can accept that the world is round would completely knock you off your axis.[18] Advancing our own knowledge requires us to be open to challenging some of our core beliefs, and that can be a very uncomfortable experience.

---

17. Originally outlined in his 1943 paper *A Theory of Human Motivation*, published in the Psychological Review, Abraham Maslow proposed that human needs exist on a hierarchy, with the physical needs for survival at the bottom and more psychological needs toward the top. The base level includes needs like food, water, warmth, and rest, and then is followed by safety, belonging/love, self-esteem, and finally, self-actualization.

18. Pun partially intended.

Within a narrow, day-to-day perspective, it is much easier to avoid, deny, and resist new information than it is to evolve and change. As time goes on, however, these denials add up to an unbalanced perspective that brings you further out of touch with reality. Discomfort is a necessary condition for educational advancement, for achieving balance, and for meeting the challenges of a quickly changing world. Over time, the process of rebalancing after an educational disruption will become less painful as you develop the tools to cope with and make the most out of evolution and change.

People's minds are also often closed to the hard work of self-exploration and understanding about how others function because the reputation of these activities has been sullied by one-size-fits-all, check-the-box "leadership and development" programs. When disillusioned staff hear about self-assessment tools and personal improvement journeys, they think about trust falls and bean-bag-tossing exercises. They quickly close their minds off to the possibility of doing the necessary work, intentionally refusing to get anything out of the experience.

To embrace lifelong learning, you need to be curious, which is an essential element of a balanced approach to life and, by extension, your work. To be truly curious, you must set your ego aside so you can objectively compare the benefits of "the way it's always been done" to other approaches that are equally, if not more, viable. Of course, being too curious can be disastrous. (There's a reason why it killed the cat.) However, not being curious enough drags you back down into a fixed mindset, closing you off to new information, ideas, and approaches.

I strongly recommend starting with assessment tools—such as the Myers-Briggs Type Indicator (MBTI®), DiSC® Profile, and Hogan Personality Inventory—to help facilitate a deeper understanding of the self and, by extension, others. These tools should be used with caution to ensure you're not placing labels on people or making excuses for bad behavior.

Instead, use your knowledge of MBTI, DiSC, and Hogan profiles to paint a higher-resolution picture of the individuals you're communicating with and how they are likely to process information. Remember this: All personality assessments provide participants with an estimate of where they lie on a spectrum. For example, introversion/extroversion is not a binary definition. I'm labeled as an introvert in MBTI, but not strongly so. In certain settings, I can be quite energized by human interactions. In others, I'm not. The spectrum matters.

Ask your team to take an honest shot at an assessment, and go into it with open ears and an open mind. It will serve as an impactful starting point because through the process they'll learn about themselves *and* how to work with other personality types.

The key here is conscious discomfort. These personality assessments aren't perfect, which is why I recommend using more than one. However, they often reveal aspects of ourselves that perhaps we didn't know or at least never articulated. We can't effectively sympathize and work with others until we gain that deeper understanding.

The Value of a Personal Continuous Improvement Journey

In my work at Kaplan, I am fortunate to be able to wake up each day and know that today, we'll make a difference. Today, we will help individuals and families improve themselves through educational opportunities of myriad variety. We will help create new credentials, degrees, badges, and pathways to greater economic and social opportunity. We will help corporations solve their skills gaps.

Doing this work gets me up in the morning and drives me throughout the day. Other than the field of health care, where you're saving lives each day, I can't think of a more noble and impactful profession than education.

Irrespective of the industry you work in, you're an educator too—it's imperative that you view yourself as a teacher and a lifelong learner. As a parent, mentor, leader, and/or community member, you can inspire those around you to be curious. Coach our young on the benefits of a balanced worldview. Work with educational institutions of all varieties to shape curricula that include a balanced menu of technical and behavioral competencies. And, for those braver than me, get involved in the political system to effect a meaningful balance between local needs and the worldview described above.

I purposefully overused the word *balance* in the preceding points because we're currently leaning so far right or left that we've lost the perspective that a well-rounded education can provide.

The old adage of "Reading, Writing, and Arithmetic" should be augmented to include a toolkit of emotional skills, such as empathy, tolerance, and diversity. Lifelong learning and professional continuous improvement journeys should certainly embrace new technical tools. However, they should also be balanced with an appropriate amount of exploration and reflection about how we treat and understand one another.

For example, as a health care practitioner, our son Brandon is constantly learning about new procedures and best practices, advancing his technical knowledge on a daily basis. In fact, what he learns in the morning might be put into practice as soon as that same afternoon. We want people like Brandon, who works in the emergency ward of a hospital and performs complicated medical procedures, to have a high degree of technical competency; I don't think you'll find too many people who would argue against that.

What we fail to acknowledge, however, is that there is often equal value in ensuring that those in highly technical fields also have a high degree of behavioral and interpersonal skills. In fact, multiple studies[19] have found that the majority of medical errors and lawsuits against medical professionals are not a result of a lapse in technical skills, but are instead the result of a miscommunication or a failure to demonstrate empathy and emotional intelligence when dealing with patients and other health care workers.

We're all teachers—all connected to the most noble of professions.[20] I'm proud to report that both of our sons are educators—Nick is a music educator and, as mentioned, Brandon is a doctor. My "ask" of you is to think of yourself as such. Viewed through this lens, our obligation to society becomes clearer. The health and longevity of Spaceship Earth depend on it.

One of the reasons why I'm writing this book is to drive home the importance of having a more balanced educational system, one that values EQ to the same degree as it does IQ. As discussed in the previous section, leaders who fail to appreciate the value of such skills ultimately contribute to a culture of disengagement, creating a clay layer that threatens a business's ability to evolve and grow. The most impactful solution is to reconsider how we train managers and leaders, and, more important, how we shed the perception that education has an age limit.

The beauty of a continuous improvement journey is that it can be truly eye opening—at least, it was for me. Adopting a continuous improvement leadership stance helped me understand how I can be a little bit better tomorrow than I was today, and how I can ensure that my mistakes and failures are viewed as opportunities to learn and grow—not as barriers to future success. I'm more open to new information, perspectives, and ideas; to being creative; and to exploring with curiosity and discovering

---

19. Most notably, *Joint Commission Perspectives*, vol. 32, no. 8 (August 2012), part of a joint commission on *Accreditation of Healthcare Organizations*, which found that "80% of serious medical errors involve miscommunication between caregivers during the transfer of patients."

20. My bias may be showing here—nurses, doctors, firefighters, police officers, and members of the military are also frequently listed as "noble professions." Education is the foundation of all the aforementioned professions, so in my mind, it comes first.

new ways of disrupting old habits that may have persisted for years, if not decades.

Once you engage in a continuous improvement journey, the pieces will begin to fall into place; it will be much easier to evaluate your own balance in life against the backdrop of where you've been, and you'll realize how to continue developing over time.

If we don't address the real resistance to change that exists in every organization, and if we don't change our cultural view toward education and lifelong learning, we will ultimately be unprepared for the new reality that is quickly approaching. It is our responsibility as leaders of businesses and communities to promote the importance and benefits of lifelong learning to our youth. We must also bring the clay layer in our organizations out from the shadows and into the daylight. We need to invest in these individuals with impactful, measurable training and engagement opportunities.

The benefits of providing mentorship and coaching to help the permafrost see the wisdom in purposeful discomfort are not to be underestimated. You have to show those among the clay layer that there's a better, different way to approach their careers; a way that will get them excited and engaged in their work again. If being purposefully uncomfortable is a necessary condition for true learning and growth, then having a coach or mentor who can lead the way is critical to the change management and learning processes.

Senior management and policy makers can talk all day about the need for change. However, the only way to make it happen is to create an army of agile problem solvers who take the challenge seriously and promote the benefits of purposeful discomfort to others in their sphere of influence.

This investment in people is the warmth that melts permafrost; it is the nutrient that helps transform clay into productive soil.

I'm proposing we draw the starting line at winning the hearts and minds of the disillusioned within our organizations by investing in their development through coaching, mentoring, and skills development. Only then can we change the culture around the role education plays in our daily lives, especially after graduation.

Four Core Competencies of a Future-Ready Workforce

Historically, individuality was not embraced at work unless you were lucky enough to be the boss, an Imagineer for Disney, a sole proprietor, or a member of a skunkworks team in the basement of a major corporation. Most of us were specialized cogs working in very big wheels. Those big wheels were driven by iconic leaders who could let their egos shine. Individuality was reserved for kings, queens, and the C-suite—not middle management or individual contributors.

Enter stage right machines that can "think" at low cognitive levels (AI), as well as a relentless need for more differentiation in increasingly crowded markets. For humans to remain relevant in the future world of work, we must encourage individuality and creative thinking. Today's consumer demands a custom, personalized experience at every turn. As machines assume more responsibility for delivering mass customization, it's our job to deliver on personalization. For the foreseeable future, only humans will be positioned to truly understand what personalization means in the markets we serve.

Likewise, there is a range of technical skills that most of us assumed we would never have to learn. Organizations were divided along strict departmental lines, valuing individual expertise in a given discipline over a diversity of skills. If you worked in the marketing department, for example, there was no need to learn about data science; that was a job for the nerds[21] down the hall. Instead, you were primarily valued for your level

---

21. The term *nerds* is used with deep affection. I'm a nerd and proud of it.

of expertise in marketing. The same was true across every department; there was no need to gain a deep understanding of your colleagues' roles if their work didn't directly overlap with your own.

Those clearly defined roles and strict divisions of labor, however, often led to interdepartmental conflict, as each group competed for resources, opportunity, and a seat at the table. Left unattended, that competitive landscape eventually led to mistrust, infighting, and an unbalanced working culture.

That is why education, mentoring, and coaching are such powerful forces for creating resilient, future-ready organizations. To activate the clay layer and bring our disillusioned team members in the moveable middle out from the shadows, we must equip them with the skills that make it easier to break down those traditional silos that facilitate an "us versus them" mindset.

Specifically, there are four key competencies that I believe everyone needs in order to work effectively across departments, understand how their individual contributions fit into the bigger picture, and ultimately thrive in a future of increasingly advanced technology.

Those four competencies are financial acumen, data literacy, commercial acumen, and human skills.

I won't dwell too much on human skills—also referred to as soft skills, EQ, and social and emotional skills—because I've already given them a spotlight in previous sections and will continue to do so moving forward.

For now, I'd like to focus on the other three hard skills that should be at the core of everyone's continuous improvement journey. I also want to highlight that I'm using the words *literacy* and *acumen* purposefully, as opposed to words like *expertise* and *mastery*. In the future, organizations will still have experts in finance, IT, human resources, sales and marketing, and so forth. However, it will be increasingly vital for every member of the organization to have some base-level competency in each of those fields.

Without some level of fluency, there will be no way for members of different departments to speak the same language, misinterpretation and competition will persist, trust will erode as interdepartmental competition rages on, and disillusionment will run rampant.

Instead, it's incumbent on leaders to engage their middle managers in a continuous improvement journey that helps them develop the skills and proficiencies that will best serve both them as individuals and the organization as a whole in the future workforce.

Financial Acumen

Operating income margin. Revenue growth. Shareholder value. Cost per lead. Capital allocation. Return on investment. Net promoter score. Capacity utilization.

Are these concepts familiar, or does the sound of them make you queasy?

From an early age, most of us are told that "math is hard" or that only certain people are "math people." As a result, we're actively discouraged from learning the language of math.[22] In many academic settings, math has been made to be mysterious and overly complex. I've personally had instructors who went out of their way to make math unapproachable—as if understanding the language of math is reserved for a special club that I needed to earn the right to enter through mental hazing and intimidation.

In reality, math is an elegant language—much more elegant and logical than English—and nearly all mathematical concepts can be directly

---

22. According to the Carnegie Foundation's 2013 study, *Pathways to Improvement*, by Elena Silva and Taylor White, 60% of America's then 13 million two-year college attendees are placed in remedial math, and 75% of them either fail or drop the course. The problem is especially acute for women. A 2016 study titled *Women 1.5 Times More Likely to Leave STEM Pipeline after Calculus Compared to Men* by Jessica Ellis, Bailey Fosdick, and Chris Rasmussen, published by PLOS ONE, found a lack of confidence, not ability, was the primary reason why women give up on STEM education.

mapped to a real-world experience. It drives me nuts when I hear people say, "I don't need to remember what they taught me in math class—I'm never going to use those concepts in real life!" What's likely happened is that those individuals had teachers who didn't connect the dots between mathematical concepts and their experiential application.

Worse yet, there's an entire swath of the population that's convinced themselves that they *can't* learn math. This is a fallacy and a crutch—as I mentioned before, math is just another language like English or Spanish. Nearly all of us have the ability to be multilingual.

The point I'm driving at is that we need to apply more effort as a society and as educators to making math more approachable and relevant. Why? Because our businesses and institutions are populated by millions who lack the necessary numeracy skills to be effective in their jobs. They've been conditioned to think that math doesn't matter in the real world when math is literally the language of business!

If math is the language of business, then everyone who works in a business should have some level of fluency in that language. Unfortunately, we live in a world where financial literacy and numeracy are at or near all-time lows. Ask the average late-Millennial or early Gen Z'er if they know how to balance a checkbook, and they'll just give you a nonplussed look of curiosity. We can turn things around, though, if we work together and embrace the following concepts.

First and foremost, we have to make mathematics more approachable and relevant in our primary and secondary schools. The latest data from the ACT show that in 2019, only 39 percent of ACT-tested high school graduates in the United States met their College Readiness Benchmark in mathematics, and this is down from 43 percent in 2014.[23]

23. *The Condition of College & Career Readiness* 2019; ACT.

We must also change the language we use with our children when we talk about math. The current vernacular that math is scary, hard, and reserved for geeks is hurting our society and economy. The beauty of mathematics is everywhere—the Fibonacci sequence shows up in many of the architectural achievements we marvel at, and fractals show up everywhere in the natural structures of plants and animals.[24]

Before we can substantially raise the bar on financial acumen, we need our next generation of business leaders to be financially literate. Again, this starts in our schools and in our homes. Just because "the computer does all the work" in banking and finance doesn't mean we shouldn't understand the mechanics of how to balance a checkbook or what debt burdens are appropriate for a particular income level.

In the business world, the adoption of a continuous improvement journey can be an effective step in ensuring that all teams are creating effective KPIs[25] to manage their part of the business. "Finance for the Non-financial Manager" programs can be useful in improving financial acumen, and education companies like Kaplan have diagnostic tools that can help assess your business's current state and measure improvement over time based on various educational interventions.

You can also start hiring with numeracy and financial acumen as a formal part of the process, even for non-math-specific roles. As employers, if we keep giving our team members a "pass" on numeracy, it won't be considered important, and nothing will change.

---

24. Further explanation and real-world examples of these concepts can be found in Jess McNally's October 2010 *Wired* magazine article, "Earth's Most Stunning Natural Fractal Patterns."

25. KPI: Key Performance Indicator. Examples include the operating income margin, call answer rates, net promoter score (NPS), product-line revenue and order growth, technical velocity or burndown measures, employee engagement scores, and so forth. Note that KPIs aren't necessarily financial and span a wide range of measurement activities.

Some of you might be asking, "Andy, what specific math skills have you found most helpful in your career?" If you're thinking about upskilling, I would focus on the following areas (in addition to basic numeracy):

- Basic statistical concepts like the mean, median, mode, variance, and standard deviation are essential to analyze and interpret datasets. The ability to properly formulate and test a hypothesis is a key skill for any decision maker.

- Probability theory usually scares most students away and is the hardest to teach because many instructors focus on the theory and not the practice. As a leader, your ability to accurately estimate the likelihood of potential outcomes from imperfect information is a huge part of your job.

- Various elements of discrete mathematics are also very useful. Set theory, basic mathematical logic, and game theory can also help with decision making.

If you are still spooked by these basic mathematical concepts, it's important that you begin the necessary work of catching up. There's no excuse for any business leader to not have developed strong financial acumen. However, perhaps the least valid excuse is the one I admit to having used in the past: a perception that we are "done" with learning after a certain age.

Data Literacy

The world today is increasingly filled with gadgets, devices, and "smart" objects, each of which collects a trove of data. Every click, every tap, every interaction with hardware and software is being recorded, and the data that results has immense power. In fact, data has surpassed oil to become the world's most valuable resource.[26]

---

26. "The world's most valuable resource is no longer oil, but data," *The Economist*, May 6, 2017.

Whether you're a small business owner or running a Fortune 500 company, you're generating more data today, relative to your size, than ever before. As a leader and an individual contributor, your ability to be creative and drive your business forward is going to rely, in large part, on how you're leveraging the troves of data that your business generates.

We now have the ability to take all of these data points—interactions with technology that reveal insights into human nature, employee sentiment, consumer preferences, buying habits, and a galaxy of others—and think practically about how to create new products, unlock parts of the value proposition by adding data to the mix, and adapt corporate strategies.

That is why a base-level understanding of data—how it works, where it comes from, what it can and can't do, how to visualize it, how to incorporate it into products and services, and how to harness its power effectively—is going to be an essential skill for employees of the future.

I'm not talking about creating or hiring more data scientists. I'm suggesting that every role within an organization—from sales and marketing to finance and human resources and beyond—will be impacted by the rise of what's referred to as "big data."

If you're in human resources, for example, it's increasingly vital that you understand the emerging field of people analytics. If you're in sales and marketing, it's important to be able to understand how data can be leveraged to produce more accurate forecasts and how it can serve as a tool for reaching customers and offering them more-personalized products and services. The list of applications goes on and on. Not a single corner of the organization, no matter its size, will be left untouched by the influence of data in the future.

Failing to understand the basic mechanics of data, or being unable to demonstrate a basic fluency in the language of data, will ultimately result in an individual feeling left out of the conversation and left behind.

Understanding the data that is being created, captured, and stored by the organization—and being able to think practically and creatively about how it can, should, and will be applied to the business—will be a core competency in the future workforce.

Commercial Acumen

One of the primary factors that ultimately leads to a team member's disengagement and disillusionment is a feeling that their contributions don't have a meaningful impact on the success of the organization. Feeling like we're part of a team that depends on our input is ultimately what drives us to show up to work each day excited to contribute.

When employees begin to feel like cogs in a machine or, worse, can't draw a clear line between their individual efforts and the success of the organization as a whole, they quickly become disillusioned and disengaged.

"Commercial viability," "go-to-market strategy," and "product-market fit" may be terms they've heard in passing, but many employees would likely struggle to define them. Just as data science was once the sole responsibility of the IT department and financial acumen was the responsibility of the accounting department, many of us have shrugged off these terms and concepts as the responsibility of someone who works down the hall.

The point is that many within businesses, institutions, and governments don't understand how the products and services they're involved in creating make it to market. They struggle to move from an inward focus—what they do on a day-to-day basis—to a much more outward focus—how their product, service, or brand interacts with the outside world.

People of all walks of organizational life have convinced themselves that their job is so unrelated to the commercial viability of the product or service that they don't get involved, don't understand how various products fit together, and certainly don't invest themselves in understanding how customers use the products they create.

Without a basic understanding of how their product or service is used "in the wild," team members are at risk of becoming unmotivated to help build on the company's reputation, brand awareness, or product-market fit. However, those who have even a base-level understanding of how they fit into the broader picture are better positioned to combine that knowledge with their unique expertise to spot inefficiencies, identify new opportunities, and help the business evolve and grow. Today such competencies are nice to have, but in the future, I believe they will become a base-level requirement.

Again, this is not to suggest that every employee should be an expert in these areas. Understanding how the activities of the organization fit together within the broader marketplace, however, can help individuals become better contributors, break down silos between departments, and rally employees around objectives that are bigger than their individual roles. Offering an unobstructed view of the bigger picture is vital to activating the clay layer. If members of the permafrost don't have basic commercial acumen, it's nearly impossible for them to see the forest for the trees.

The Results of a Continuous Improvement Journey

I don't have to look far to find an example of how organizations that equip their staff with these three core competencies—financial acumen, data literacy, and commercial acumen—can put them to use in a way that produces tangible results.

At Kaplan, parts of the company have been on a continuous improvement journey for the last seven years. A key tenet of continuous improvement is measurement. If you were to walk around our office, you would see video screens in nearly all departments that display that team's gemba board.[27] All gemba boards have a section for the team's KPIs. This forces the team to think carefully about the metrics that matter to their department and report on those metrics on a frequent basis, if not in real time.

The beauty of a gemba board is that the good, the bad, and the ugly of team and department performance are on display for everyone to see. The numbers are no longer hidden away or reserved for the elite in the business. Better yet, all team members play a role in determining departmental KPIs, updating the board, and engaging in gemba walks with management and other team members. Working more closely with the numbers, continually refining what gets measured, and understanding why we're measuring it improves the financial acumen, data literacy, and commercial acumen of the organization as a whole.

When teams and departments begin to draw a direct line between their work and the financial health of the firm, it has a tangible impact on productivity, morale, and engagement.

Solving the Leadership Shortage

When we're children, we dream of being astronauts, firefighters, dancers, movie stars, pilots, or as in my case, rock stars. Very few sit on the playground and say, "I want to be a manager when I grow up!"

Even when we're in high school or college and are honing a set of baseline career capabilities, very few of us imagine our future selves as leading teams of people or applying leadership skills as individual contributors. Most teachers and curricula are too focused on technical skill transfer to make the connection for students between the subjects they're studying

---

27. A gemba board is a physical or digital visual management tool that teams or departments use to show progress against goals, risks, challenges, wins, and trends in key performance indicators (KPIs). Gemba boards should show the actual state of the department's work and make plain both what's going well and what's not. A gemba walk is an opportunity for leaders and members of other departments to ask questions and listen intently about the team's work in a nonjudgmental, nonthreatening fashion.

and the behavioral skills they will need to effectively apply those concepts in the real world.

I stress that leaders can be both managers of teams and individual contributors because the ability to *influence* is a key to success, and influence is an essential leadership quality. Sometimes, you can influence by being the smartest person in the room who consistently comes up with the correct answer (the application of technical skill). But more often than not, influencers are critical thinkers, effective communicators, steady under pressure, empathetic, and collaborative—all behavioral skills that get ignored or minimized during our schooling. The result is a shortage of leadership candidates who have the skills necessary to be highly effective future managers.[28] Not many pundits are discussing leadership as a part of the skills-gap debate, and the shortage of skilled leaders at all levels needs to enter the conversation.

Now you might be saying, "What about the MBA degree as a solution?" The original intent of the MBA degree was to be an early- to mid-career top-up credential for those who hold undergraduate degrees and have an established business track record. It's for individual contributors and managers who are making a conscious decision to become well-rounded business leaders.

Unfortunately, the cost of a quality MBA makes it prohibitively expensive for most individuals with management aspirations to attain this signal of management competence. Worse yet, many MBA programs have deviated from the original intent and instead pile on more specialized technical skills than the behavioral skills that are necessary to be a successful leader. MBA programs are too often focused on cranking out road warriors for

---

28. A 2016 survey of 500 managers by SaaS learning platform Grovo titled *Good Manager, Bad Manager* found that 44% of managers felt unprepared for the role, and 87% wish they had received more training.

consulting firms or watering down admissions standards and curricula to fill back rows—neither of which helps solve the leadership shortage.[29]

Some would argue that corporations are stepping up to fill the void left by the educational system when it comes to grooming our future leaders. It's true that some companies have well-thought-out management training programs, but the reality is that truly effective programs are few and far between. Budget constraints and senior leader turnover/whims at most organizations create an environment where training is the first thing to go when things get financially tight. Also, "flavor of the day" syndrome kicks in so that most management training ends up being a loose patchwork of programming that is not tied directly and consistently to the outcomes that matter to the employee and the company.

So if everyone can't get a quality MBA and the credential has been watered down or has deviated from its original intent, what should we do to create great leaders who will drive better outcomes and business results? In the short term, senior leaders at corporations can commit to protecting learning and development budgets from the ebbs and flows of the economic cycle—at least those programs that are core to creating the leadership teams needed for future success, innovation, and sustainability. Behavioral skill development should be viewed as a must-have for business success, not a nice-to-have. Also, senior teams should invest time and money to partner with learning experts to develop leadership programs that map the curriculum to organizational "great place" outcomes and long-term business objectives.

Importantly, these programs should be designed in such a way that they are inoculated from fads and the latest trends. I'm not suggesting that programs should be immutable and rigid. Rather, they should exhibit the

---

29. If my assessment of the current state of the MBA program strikes a nerve and prompts a more robust discussion on the future of this credential, the purpose of including it in this book will have been achieved.

right balance between consistency and the need to flex as the business changes and grows.

In the long term, our teachers and school administrators should also commit to learning more about the behavioral aspects of workplace success for the subjects they teach.

At an early age, students should be able to make the connection between the technical skills they're acquiring and the behavioral skills they will need for their work to be truly impactful. This won't be easy, but by applying more team-oriented experiential learning techniques to the classroom, teachers can demonstrate to students much earlier that success is derived from being able to work in high-functioning teams where communication, trust, and collaboration are essential. By engaging in this work, we'll have fewer unskilled "accidental managers" and more students who grow up to embrace the benefits of understanding how to influence and lead.

I count myself as one of these accidental managers—both my team members and I could have benefited greatly from a more balanced technical/behavioral approach.

Another long-term impact that teachers and mentors can have on narrowing the skills gap is in helping to instill a sense of personal responsibility for lifelong learning into the individuals they're coaching. In my opinion, monolithic credentials, such as the degree and diploma, give the future stewards of our planet the idea that they're somehow done learning when they graduate.

I certainly used to think this way when I was a young man and couldn't wait to be done with my schooling—then I would be able to move on to whatever was coming next. What I didn't realize at the time was that a journey of continuous improvement and lifelong learning was what came next. Unfortunately, I purposely avoided some educational opportunities early in my career because I had convinced myself that I had acquired enough education, that I was "done."

I've seen way too many young men and women look with dread at their next learning opportunity. Unfortunately, the root cause for this behavior is primarily the negative or skeptical attitudes exhibited within our core family units toward the benefits of education. Today, we have enough evidence that education is one of the best investments individuals can make for themselves and their families. To be clear, college and advanced degrees aren't for everyone. But *everyone* should adopt a positive attitude toward continuous personal and professional improvement by being curious, lifelong learners—embracing educational opportunities in real time as they progress through their careers.

Teachers and mentors (parents specifically) are critical in changing attitudes toward personal growth through education. The leadership shortage I describe will become much less acute if we all do our part to promote the benefits of lifelong learning, balance education between technical and human skills, and begin leaning into the upcoming Reskilling Revolution.

PART 3
Effective Communication

When I was eight years old, I played Arne in a collegiate production of *I Remember Mama*—a morality play that follows an immigrant Norwegian family in the early twentieth century. Arne is a bit player who suffers from a fractured kneecap—one of several challenges the family must overcome as the parents try to educate their children so they can lead a better life.

One of the more influential characters in the play is Mama's Uncle Chris. Uncle Chris's character is a stern, crotchety Norwegian man. So it's natural that the children, especially Arne, are intimidated by him. As you might expect, though, Uncle Chris has a softer, playful side as well. In my "big scene," Uncle Chris is helping Arne deal with the pain he is experiencing from his injuries and teaches Arne some swear words as a distraction.

"Do you know any swear words?" asks Uncle Chris. Arne feigns to not know any. Uncle Chris coaches Arne that if the pain gets bad, he should use the words *damn* and *damnittohell* to relieve the pain.

Of course, I needed to practice my lines at home so I could be prepared for rehearsal. Now imagine eight-year-old Andy running around the house yelling, "Damn, damn, damnittohell!" over and over and over again. It drove my parents nuts.

The reason for introducing you to eight-year-old Andy and my first theatrical escapade is because it was my first exposure to storytelling. Certainly, my parents read me stories, and I had been to various children's productions, but this was the first time I was telling a coherent story with a team of other storytellers to a large audience. I had no way of knowing at the time that storytelling would become an important part of my career—first as a teacher and then as an executive and leader. In fact, storytelling ranks at, or near, the top of the list of critical skills I have developed over the years.

Setting strategy and corporate direction is a bit like writing a play. The playwright needs to set a context-appropriate stage that a diverse team of performers, designers, and production personnel can connect with; identify meaningful characters and roles; and weave a story that the audience can relate to and is interested in buying. Most important, the story must hold together such that logical inconsistencies are minimized and the relationships between characters are coherent. A good play (in my humble opinion) is balanced, neither too long nor too short—it also avoids unnecessary complexity that detracts from the main theme.

Uniqueness is an essential characteristic of a good play, but it too requires an element of balance—audience members tend to like a product that strikes equilibrium between the familiar and the unexpected.[1] Too much differentiation and a product is likely to be considered ahead of its time and not meet with economic success. Too little differentiation and the result will be bland and vanilla.

In a business setting, the corporate story (strategy) must undergo continual refinement. The time commitment to strategy setting is considerable

---

1. Just look at Broadway's biggest hit in recent years, *Hamilton.*

and is typically greater than most new leaders expect. Unlike a classic, long-running theatrical production, the corporate story is constantly under attack from new competitors, shifting consumer tastes and preferences, fickle government regulations, and demographic/generational shifts. Therefore, fighting entropy is critical. If the corporate story is left unattended too long, it will begin to atrophy and deteriorate as internal politics, egos, and competing priorities chip away at it.

After you've written the story, it needs to be told. But before you can tell it, the acting roles must be cast, responsibilities for the crew established, marketing and promotion strategies created, and resources allocated—all with impeccable timing.

I'm not going to get into the details of day-to-day strategy execution. What's important now is for us to concentrate on "right person, right role." In a theatrical production, great care is taken to cast actors for each role. We've all seen plays or movies where the casting wasn't quite right. Instead of getting immersed in the scene, we're wondering why on Earth the casting director chose *him*?

In business, you can set the most beautiful strategy, but if you don't have the right players to execute it, you're going nowhere. Even more important, as strategy changes, the players need to change too. One of my biggest failings as a leader over the years has been to assume that the players who were hired to execute our strategy were still the right players for that strategy five years later.

This is why talent acquisition and talent development are so important to a business. A talent management program that is in lockstep with the corporate story is essential for proper execution. It's our responsibility as leaders to identify potential skill gaps in our team members and provide development opportunities to help them succeed as priorities shift. However, this responsibility is not one-way.

Team members also have the responsibility of continuously learning and engaging in constructive conversations with their leaders about the skills and competencies needed by the organization in the future. As outlined in part 2, lifelong learning should be a continual process of forecasting skill gaps, remediating those gaps, and ensuring that the needs of the individual contributor align with the needs of the business. If those needs begin to diverge, "right person, right role" conversations should commence, and an exit from the organization may be necessary. However, upskilling and/or reskilling should be the top priority.

Although these "fit and fitness" discussions can be difficult, an exit from the organization could be the best thing for both parties. Playing a role that no longer fits you or the company only creates discord, tension, and unnecessary emotional and physical waste.

The output of the strategy-setting process provides the inputs for the performances you put on in the next year. You've crafted the story, so now it needs to be told. In the collegiate production of *I Remember Mama*, in which I played Arne, we performed the play on one stage over two weeks to substantially similar audiences. In business, the story must be told across geographies, cultures, and demographics using multiple modalities.

The old marketing adage, the "rule of seven," says you have to say something seven times for a message to get across. I would alter this adage to "you have to say things seven ways through seven modalities" for the message to be received and for teams to begin the climb up the change management curve.[2]

---

2. There are many varieties of change management curves. Kotter and Prosci are two examples.

In my previous roles at Kaplan, I wrote my annual letter to staff, delivered four town halls per year, engaged in skip-level[3] meetings, produced video interview segments with other senior team members, and held monthly board meetings with department executives. Those are just a few modalities we employed to reinforce messages, and I still felt I wasn't doing enough.

I used to believe I could say something once and the team would get it. How incredibly lazy and naïve I was. I learned later that I should have been using my storytelling skills to develop a rich portfolio of opportunities for my team members to understand the direction we were headed. I realize now that communication is very much a two-way street and that I must do more to tailor messages to where team members are on the change curve—to meet them where they're at.

This certainly doesn't absolve team members from their individual responsibility to be aware of and understand what's going on around them. However, a leader must be more situationally and emotionally aware than their team members. As a leader, you must recognize that every time you engage in a conversation with someone else, the other party has already established their own narrative and is likely in a very different place in the conversation than you are.

The story must also be consistent and persistent. If the story you're telling is constantly changing or is infrequently told, the audience will begin to tune out and revert to its own narrative—a narrative that's very likely aligned with "the way we've always done it" because the familiar is more comfortable than the unknown, especially when the unknown is not well-defined. So if you scratch your head and wonder why your teams don't seem to be on the same journey as you, take a look at how consis-

---

3. A skip-level meeting is where a leader meets with members of their direct-report's teams—typically without the direct report present—to listen to the challenges and opportunities faced by the team. Skip-level meetings remove the potential bias of a layer of management and allow leaders to get a clearer picture of the team's work.

tent and persistent you've been in your communication. Consistency and persistence will help build the trust that's vital to a healthy organization.

I've been a performer most of my life—child actor, singer, musician, teacher, and business leader. It wasn't until later in my career that I connected the dots on how my experience as a performer was benefiting my life in business. I'm not recommending that you take up acting classes or join a band in order to be a better leader, but honing your skill as a multimodality storyteller can certainly pay dividends. More important, I ask you to reflect on the last time you told your corporate story. Are you telling it enough and in varied ways? Storytelling can be scary, but just like any other muscle, it needs to be strengthened and exercised.

Lastly, it's not just the responsibility of the CEO to tell the story. All leaders and contributors in the organization should be able to tell the corporate story. In a healthy organization, these stories all align, are consistent, and hold together.

Oh, and if you see me muttering to myself after a difficult meeting, I'm not losing my mind: I'm just reciting my old line: *damn, damn, damnittohell.*

Listen Up

Businesses are made up of people, and the success of businesses relies on how those people interact, communicate, and collaborate with each other. Today, we have access to more tools and modes of communication and collaboration than ever before, yet we still struggle to understand one another, to *hear* each other, and to get our messages across effectively.

Ironically, as our communication tools get more sophisticated, our language often moves in the opposite direction. Today, the average Gen Z'er or Millennial is probably more familiar with emoticons, emojis, and giphys than with proper spelling, grammar, sentence structure, and punctuation. I don't mean to pick on younger generations; they were simply the first to be raised in a world of social media and instant messaging. Many members of my generation demonstrate similar challenges with language.

Whatever generation you belong to, it's likely that you were never taught about effective communication in school. Every student in the English-speaking world is required to gain a certain proficiency in their native language, but there is so much more to communication than improving one's vocabulary. Unless you pursued further education in a field that explicitly required better-than-average communication skills—such as marketing, sales, or corporate communications—you likely stopped advancing those skills at a relatively young age.

With communication taking a back seat to most other skills and competencies in our education system, it's no wonder that we're still struggling with issues of misunderstanding and miscommunication in the world, both within the workplace and beyond.

Just as a couple's counselor will emphasize the difference between *hearing* one's partner speak and *actively listening* to what one's partner is saying, our society is awash in one-way communication tools—thanks to ubiquitous access to digital megaphones—which drive increased polarization. In business, in politics, in spousal relationships and beyond, we fail to listen because we make assumptions, because our egos get in the way, because we take something or someone for granted, or because we've closed our minds to being challenged, whether consciously or not.

The epidemic of disengagement that plagues businesses of all shapes and sizes can almost always be traced back to some sort of failure of communication: failing to respond to important requests in a timely manner, failing to respond to critical feedback, failing to acknowledge those who deserve recognition, and/or failing to address a difficult subject. When you take the time to really investigate how or why employees lost the light in their eyes, how they became disengaged from their work, or how they became part of the clay layer that's resistant to change, you usually find that a lapse in effective communication is almost always the culprit.

Hiding behind instant, text-based communication and social media—where we can literally block opinions that make us feel uncomfortable—has conditioned us to write people off in the real world. Instead, we make assumptions, avoid difficult conversations, and choose to ignore rather than to listen. The same happens in business too. Often, managers seem better prepared to deal with the complexity and cost of hiring someone new than to have a difficult but necessary conversation with an existing team member.

For example, let's say Steve is asked by his boss, Amy, to write up a report for the CEO. Amy provides very clear instructions to Steve on how he should proceed, but Steve decides to be bold and go in a different direction. He hands the report to the CEO, who is displeased with the end result. Steve made a mistake, but Amy was the one who got reprimanded by the CEO for failing to teach Steve how to do his job properly.

Rather than confronting Steve about the challenges with the report and offering some coaching to help him improve, Amy makes the assumption that Steve is unreliable. Amy swears she'll never trust him to write another report again.

Years go by, Steve matures in his development, he learns from his previous mistakes, and he believes he now knows how to write a report that will impress his CEO, but it's no use. Amy has already written Steve off; her ego won't let her accept that Steve has changed. She's built a narrative in her head that says, "Steve is incapable of writing reports," and refuses to be challenged in that assumption. The sting of the embarrassment she felt that day still lingers years later.

Rather than help Steve improve his skills and advance his career, Amy decides that it is simply beyond Steve's capacity and any training or development provided to him would be wasted. Once Steve realizes that he doesn't have a future with the company, he becomes disillusioned. The light in his eye diminishes, and he begins looking for work elsewhere. If only Amy had been willing to have that difficult conversation about Steve's mistakes in the first place, she would have retained an employee that had some real potential. Instead, she feels relief at the thought that Steve—that terrible employee who embarrassed her *once* in front of the CEO many years ago—is finally leaving the company.

Rather than addressing difficult subjects head-on, we've been conditioned to take the easy way out. We exist in a world where, unless we live in a very small community, we don't have to interact with those we decide we don't like or don't agree with. We are quick to judge others, and when we deem someone not worth our time, we cut them out. We desperately need to get better at listening to one another and at receiving information openly and willingly, rather than blocking out voices that make us feel uncomfortable.

I come to this subject honestly as an introvert and a long-time conflict avoider who spent too much time hearing without actually *listening*. People like me—and there are millions of us—would prefer to let things that cause us pain or discomfort slide versus addressing them head-on. However, as someone who has been down that road many times, I can assure you that letting things slide leads to nowhere but trouble.

Failing to stand up and voice concern or objection out of fear of discomfort provides implicit and/or explicit approval of something we don't agree with. If we fail to find our voices in those moments, the subjects, opinions, and conflicts we've avoided only calcify and become more difficult to solve in the future. By not speaking up, we open the door to false assumptions. Amy didn't tell Steve what he did wrong, but Steve can sense that he's lost his manager's trust and assumes Amy just has it out for him. Steve didn't get the chance to explain himself and why he made that bold but ultimately unwise choice, so Amy assumes he's incompetent. They spend years assuming the worst of each other while avoiding a difficult but necessary conversation that could resolve everything.

We avoid such conversations because we build narratives in our heads about how they will likely go, and those fictions almost never come to fruition. It's like working out. When most of us consider the prospect of going to the gym, we are filled with dread. Those of us who actually make it there on occasion, though, know that after a workout we almost always feel better.

The same is true of difficult conversations. We often go into them with dread, but we leave with a sense of satisfaction. In most instances, we discover that the conflict was based on a simple misunderstanding, that the other party was much more open to hearing a hard truth than we had assumed, or that both parties were already on the same page but never articulated it.

Having been through countless difficult conversations myself, I know that most will come to a satisfactory conclusion. Yet I still can't help but feel nervous going into them; it's just human nature. Our brains have been conditioned to react in a way that causes us to avoid danger and potential conflict rather than confront it. When we give into that fear, it's often at the expense of reason and logic, which is ultimately what separates us from nearly all other species on the planet.

Indulge me for a moment; let's say that there's a horse who stands under a tree every day to shield himself from the hot sun. One day, while standing under that familiar tree, a monkey falls from one of its branches and startles the horse.

Here in Wisconsin, the likelihood of another monkey falling out of the tree in the foreseeable future is near zero. Regardless of how unlikely that situation is to repeat itself, I can assure you that the horse will never stand under his favorite tree again. That tree will forever bear the markings of a negative association in his mind. It's now the "monkey tree."

While the horse is unlikely to ever visit that tree again of his own accord, a skilled trainer can use positive association techniques to retrain the horse to use the tree as shade. If enough positive *reactions* accumulate, the horse will return to the shade of the tree.

What separates us from the animals is that we have the ability to apply *reason* and *logic* to the "monkey in the tree" example. Although it might be scary or uncomfortable at first, we can learn *on our own* to trust that spot under the tree again. Unfortunately, I don't see as many humans using their reasoning abilities as I would hope. More often, we take the more animalistic, reactionary approach to difficult situations because it's easier than confronting a potentially scary or uncomfortable scenario.

"Why should I take the risk if I can just avoid the tree with the monkey in it? After all, there are plenty of other trees out there, and none of *them* make me feel uncomfortable. It would be much easier to ignore that tree and pretend it doesn't exist."

Amy decided that she will never trust Steve with another report again. It doesn't matter how long ago the incident took place or how much Steve has developed since then. Amy has closed herself off to reason and made assumptions about Steve; now it's a matter of ego. If Steve *does* prove to be a valuable employee with lots to offer, that would reflect poorly on Amy, the manager who failed to identify and nurture Steve's talent. As a result, Amy is invested in seeing Steve fail, which would prove to everyone that she was right about Steve all along.

This is, of course, not a real story, but it is representative of a dynamic that is far too common in today's workplace. Businesses are made up of people, and, in order to succeed, those people need to be able to *hear* one another, have difficult but necessary conversations, *listen* to logic and reason, and have the strength to set their egos aside. I'm asking you to take an evolutionary step forward and defer to reason rather than reaction.

In previous sections, I've discussed the importance of behavioral skills like emotional intelligence, empathy, and trust. Here, I want to talk about the place where all of those individual skills and capabilities intersect: in how we communicate with one another.

Miscommunication in our personal lives can destroy relationships, just as miscommunication in the workplace can destroy careers, business opportunities, partnerships, client relationships, sales prospects, and economic value. If we are able to bridge the gap in communication skills by even a few degrees, the value creation to society would be immense.

As with other skills and competencies highlighted thus far, communication has historically been brushed off as secondary or important only to those whose roles specifically require such skills. I believe that effective communication, however, is a base-level requirement for addressing the clay layer, for fighting the epidemic of disengagement, and for creating a more balanced workplace.

The Difference Between Music and Noise

Noise /noiz/ (noun): *any sound that is undesired or interferes with one's hearing of something*[4]

When I was a young man, I would sit in the basement of our home with a friend or two and blast Molly Hatchet's "Flirtin' with Disaster"[5] as loudly as the stereo would go (and yes, it was a vinyl album on a turntable with gigantic speakers). Those of you who know the genre can picture the scene—sweaty teenage boys running around with air guitars and air

---

4. https://www.merriam-webster.com/dictionary/noise
5. Epic Records, 1979.

drums, totally rockin' out. Invariably, one of my parents would shout down the stairs, "Turn down that noise!" To me, it was music–appropriate for my age and disposition at that time of my life. To my parents, it was noise.

I wore the grooves off many such albums by bands like Rush, Kansas, Supertramp, and Styx, and drove my parents bananas in the process. In retrospect, had I been more mature, I would have taken the time to explain why my music was important to me in a constructive, objective manner.

Equally, it was their responsibility as adults to try to see the world through my lens instead of simply writing off this new music as a scourge in our society. Looking at the same material through different filters and not working to understand how those filters functioned led to unnecessary conflict in our home.

In my late teens, I owned a pair of rose-colored glasses–I thought I was so cool when I had them on, and to a certain extent they defined my personal brand at the time. We all walk around with a set of lenses through which we look at the world. Our lenses have been colored by our education, families, and work experiences–they are unique to each of us and help define our worldview.

Importantly, the "color" of your lenses changes over time and with experience. If I had to wear glasses today, they would probably have a light blue tint to them, which represents my current view–logical, balanced, and optimistic. As an individual on a continuous improvement journey, I am committed to ensuring my lenses improve in clarity and resolution as I age.

Earlier in my career, I was on a team project with a man with whom I had been acquainted for years–let's call him Sam. Once we started working together–having substantive conversations–I quickly realized that when Sam spoke, I had difficulty processing what he was talking about. At first I tried to decipher his intent but rapidly became frustrated with our inability to communicate effectively. Sam's words had turned to noise in my ears, and I did what most people do with noise—I shut it out.

Ultimately, our relationship deteriorated to the point where I would purposely avoid interacting with him unless I absolutely had to. As a result, the project we were working on failed. It was a true failure because we didn't learn from the experience. Instead, team members blamed each other, creating an unhealthy work environment and fueling mistrust and resentment that was left unaddressed. This project team worked on a few additional projects over the next few years with limited results. Ultimately, Sam left the company, and a great deal of potential business value was never realized—all because my voice was noise to Sam, and his voice was certainly noise to me.

Sam is not a particularly remarkable character in my life story. However, he is one that created a memorable amount of angst and stress that could have been avoided had I done a bit more work and opened my mind to other ways of thinking. Specifically, what this earlier version of Andy didn't realize was that I had an obligation to understand the lens through which Sam viewed the world. Arrogance, ego, and overt resistance to any type of behavioral training led me to believe that my viewpoint was all that mattered. My closed mind caused me to hear noise when Sam spoke. If I could have seen Sam through the tint of today's light-blue glasses and made a real effort to consider the lenses through which he saw me, things would have probably played out much differently.

Unfortunately, I see versions of this story unfold frequently in business. Closed minds, narrow worldviews, and a general lack of willingness or ability among team members to invest the time and energy needed to think about the impact of lenses on team dynamics can be a leading cause of organizational discord. Lenses are not one size fits all; they're *one size fits you*. Hence, we must be mindful that our perspective is unique, and we must help others understand how our lenses color and distort incoming information. I think of this coloration and distortion as the "Lensing Effect."

What can you do to minimize the Lensing Effect? First, actively work to understand yourself and your coworkers. The Myers-Briggs Type Indicator (MBTI),[6] Hogan Assessments,[7] and DiSC Profile[8] mentioned in part 2 of this book are examples of personality assessments that can be used to gain a better understanding of your own lens and the lenses your coworkers look through. Use your knowledge of MBTI, DiSC, and Hogan to paint a higher-resolution picture of the individuals you're communicating with and how they are likely to process information.

Second, diversify your message. As mentioned earlier, it often takes more than seven times to get a message through. You also must communicate the message through multiple channels and in different ways. If your message is being received as noise, saying it slower or louder won't help.

Third, focus on the importance of the "why." No matter how wonderful you are as a communicator or how liked you are within the organization, crisply communicating the "why" behind your message is critical. This is because the status quo in most mature organizations is skepticism. Unless you're incredibly charismatic and have your teams under a spell, you'll need to present the "why" behind a decision or proposal in order to reduce the noise around your message and increase its fidelity.

Finally, seek to improve your listening skills. Active *listening*—rather than passive *hearing*—is key to gaining understanding in a conversation. Far too often I find myself thinking about how to phrase my rebuttal instead of understanding meaning and context and interpreting the body language of the person I'm talking to. I've got a long way to go here—

---

6. https://www.myersbriggs.org
7. https://www.hoganassessments.com
8. https://www.discprofile.com

especially on a personal level with those I love the most. I can't tell you how many times I've disappointed my spouse by not being "present," causing me to forget key details of our conversations. Put down the phone, unplug, and listen. When you truly listen, you might find music where there was once the perception of noise.

I haven't turned my parents into raving fans of what we now call classic rock, but they have found an appreciation for it because they know how meaningful it is to me. They can understand its greater context and the influence it had in molding me as a person. Put in a business context, they made time and expended energy to hear and understand my point of view. My perspective hasn't miraculously become theirs, but we've learned that through constructive discourse, we can appreciate each other's music and points of view. Think about your network, both past and present—it's highly likely that you can identify a "Sam" in your life.

Remember, your lens is one size fits you. Everyone sees things differently.

Why Email Is the Worst

Ten years from now, if anyone reads this book, they'll say something like, "Look, Jimmy, here's a section that talks about email! How quaint." However, until the time email is supplanted by more effective communication tools, its use in business creates tremendous challenges we must work to overcome.

I am personally at the age where I've seen email grow from an oddity to the predominant form of corporate communication. We currently live in a time of disruption as other collaboration tools, such as Slack and Zoom, gain prominence and slowly unseat email from its dominant position. The pandemic has accelerated their rise, but it will be a long time before they overtake email as our primary workplace communication tool. So how do we make the best of the tools we have today?

Specifically, in my position, I am either directly involved in, or am an observer to, significant corporate value destruction that can be directly tied to the improper use of email and other one-way communication tools. Certainly, email can help build value by reinforcing effective communications (e.g., a confirmatory information exchange or announcement). However, my hypothesis is that we're at an inflection point where email may be destroying more value than it adds.

Let's look at a quick example. Your business just landed a new partnership with WizzyWidget, Inc., that promises to generate significant revenue and operating income for the company. Suzie and Billy manage two separate departments that must work together to support the partnership with WizzyWidget properly. They both understand the importance of the relationship but have differing opinions about how to support this new line of business. Suzie and Billy haven't dedicated enough effort to understanding the lens through which the other sees the world. Although they've been trained on the need for direct and constructive challenging conversations, they tend to revert to communication via email. As the "tennis match" of emails goes back and forth between these leaders, unnecessary tension grows, deliverables for the partnership slip, and ultimately, the partnership fails—destroying corporate value. Fingers are then pointed by both parties in myriad directions, and no one is held accountable for the failure. Worse yet, the teams don't learn from it.

Sound familiar? I'm sure if you sit quietly for a few minutes and dig in the recesses of your mind, you'll come up with similar examples: the energy-sapping overuse of "reply all"; the two team members who work in the same department but never talk directly with one another and communicate exclusively electronically; the hastily written communications that delay action because they require further clarification; and so on.

Unfortunately, we spend almost no time helping our peers and coworkers build effective one-way communication skills. It is indeed a skill required to get the most value from email—a skill typically overlooked because it's viewed as too mundane or low level to warrant the airplay it really deserves.

Clearly, in the example above, if Billy and Suzie had been aware that their passive-aggressive behaviors were harming the business, they may have acted differently. In many cases, participants in email chains like this are operating on autopilot and allowing their subconscious mind to select the mode and style of communication.

My recommendation is that we treat email with respect and think consciously about the circumstances under which one-way communication is beneficial (right tool, right job) and when it is likely to be disruptive. Specifically, I recommend adopting the following three rules that can help facilitate more effective one-way communication over email.

1. **Rule #1**

    When in doubt, pick up the phone—or better yet, use video-based collaboration tools when face-to-face isn't an option. Would you really say what you've written if you were face-to-face with the recipient? It's amazing how brash and brazen people can be when they know the other party can't immediately respond and isn't looking into their eyes. To check yourself here, imagine you have to stand directly in front of the intended recipient and make eye contact as you read the contents of your email aloud. Would you still choose email as the communication format? If the use of email is unavoidable, would you use the same words?

2. **Rule #2**

    Establish a cooling-off period. For particularly sensitive matters, take the time to let a response rest—even a thirty-minute rest can make the difference between sending a destructive communication and sending one that adds value. This pause will allow you to consider whether you're using the right communication tool and/or whether what you've written has the potential to be misinterpreted by the recipient. Too many of us get caught in the trap where we believe we have to respond immediately to email. This leads to poor decision making and less-than-optimal communication. Before hitting "send," let the email simmer in your drafts folder and return to it after you've had a few moments to collect yourself.

3. Rule #3

Check for tone, and practice your emotional intelligence skills. Put yourself in the recipient's shoes, and listen for how your tone might be interpreted. You can say exactly the same thing to two different people and get completely different reactions. This is due to how you say the words and how those words are filtered through the recipient's lens.

These rules aren't specific to business communication either; they can also help in managing personal relationships, especially in times of high stress (e.g., separation or divorce). I can personally attest that engaging in a fight over email seldom ends well.

Let me get on my soapbox now. The worst kinds of one-way communications are anonymous online comments and reactions to news stories in your local online newspaper. If you're going to add your voice in the public realm, be courageous, attach your name to the comment, and most of all, be constructive. Don't be "that" guy or gal who anonymously bullies or tosses grenades into a conversation without offering constructive solutions.

We all have our own lens through which we view the world. This lens colors how we see and interpret the world around us—especially language and communication. As an example, a good friend might ask, "Where were *you* last night?" You might interpret the question as a genuine request to start a conversation about your evening. However, if your spouse asked the same question, "Where *were* you last night?" your response might be completely different based on your accumulated prior experience and how the sentence was phrased.

Unlike direct voice communication, where interpretation of emphasis and nuance is more straightforward, an email leaves interpretation completely in the hands of the recipient. This significantly increases the risk of misinterpretation and conflict.

In the crush of daily business, email and other one-way communication tools can create great organizational efficiency to consistently ensure team members all hear the same thing at the same time. Email can also destroy tremendous amounts of shareholder value and damage organizational health if used inappropriately.

There have been many situations during my career where I've lamented, in retrospect, over my choice of email to communicate sensitive or mission-critical topics. I've seen projects fail over petty disputes that arise from the improper use of the email medium—specifically its role as an enabler of passive-aggressive behaviors. Had I exercised just a little foresight and been more courageous, the outcome of the engagement or project could have been very different.

Email will be a part of our business lives for the foreseeable future. As leaders, let's coach our teams on the benefits and challenges of one-way communication tools. The next time you hear of someone "banging out emails," ask if they took the time to think about context and interpretation by the recipient—odds are they haven't.

Responsiveness: The Neglected Leadership Trait

We're all guilty of it—guilty of knowingly delaying a response to a colleague who was in need of advice, input to a work stream, or a decision for a project. Some might justify this behavior by convincing themselves that they're really busy and don't have time to respond. Others have hierarchy in mind and respond immediately to supervisors but will delay responses to peers and subordinates. In my case, if a response is delayed, I'm usually collecting data or allowing information I've already collected to coalesce into a well-informed decision.

You might be thinking, "Why is this important? A delay in responding isn't the end of the world!" As I continue my personal continuous improvement journey, it's dawned on me that this behavior can significantly erode interpersonal and team trust. It breeds uncertainty, puts people on edge, and can throw your team off balance. Viewed through this lens, striking the right balance in responsiveness is of critical importance to team cohesion and how others view you as a leader.

Here's a quick example:[9] A while back, division head Carol went out on a limb and wrote a memo describing a prospective structural change that would make the business more efficient, reduce costs, and potentially improve the client experience. The organizational change Carol was recommending would have been challenging to implement on a number of levels but could have really pushed the business forward. Carol had discussed this idea previously with her boss, and he encouraged her to put the idea in writing. Carol submitted the carefully crafted note via email, waited a week, and then reached out again to see if he'd received it. Still no reply. After one more receipt request, Carol gave up and assumed he

---

9. All characters are fictional, but this is a very realistic scenario with an all-too-common outcome.

wasn't interested in her work. Oddly, Carol's supervisor reached out to her on several other issues over this time period and mentioned nothing about the memo.

A month went by. During that time, Carol's supervisor was processing—thinking about how he could implement the idea with minimal disruption and maximum effect—but Carol and the handful of team members who helped her with the report were becoming increasingly nervous. "What if he didn't like the report?" "What if he's thinking about restructuring our department instead?" "What if our jobs are at risk?" As time passed, the uncertainty escalated. Finally, during a one-on-one, Carol mustered up the courage to ask directly if he'd received the report. He indicated that he had indeed received it but was busy working on other things and couldn't get to it.

Although an extreme example, her boss's behavior was more the norm than the exception. As a result, Carol became disenchanted in her role and left the business—believing that her opinion didn't matter and her boss didn't care. Oddly, Carol's supervisor was very interested in the proposal; he was delaying his response until he could truly invest himself in its contents and give it the attention it deserved. Had he quickly responded to the initial request with, "Thank you for sending me the report we talked about, but I am focused on several deadline-specific priorities and promise to respond in a few weeks," a valued employee may not have left the business. Recruiting costs, training costs, and general business disruption would have been avoided by investing thirty seconds in a brief but timely response with the appropriate follow-through.

The point is that we should all periodically grade ourselves on our level of responsiveness to ensure we're not unnecessarily engaging in behavior that's creating a challenging work environment for others and eroding both trust and accountability.

If you're finding responsiveness to be a challenge, you may want to search for the root cause in the following areas:

- **delegation** (do I know how to delegate in order to motivate and achieve successful outcomes?),

- **decision-making** (should I invest in building better decision-making muscles?),

- **time management** (have I taken on too much and need to rebalance my priorities? Am I working on the right things?),

- **constructive confrontation** (do I struggle with engaging in frank and fearless conversations?), and

- **authority and control** (am I using a lack of responsiveness as a passive-aggressive tool to show everyone who's boss?).

Please note that I'm not suggesting we need to respond *immediately* to every issue. Expecting immediate responses or trying to live up to an expectation of immediate response is unhealthy and unsustainable. Being responsive does not imply immediacy.

Striking the right balance across the points listed above will help you improve responsiveness. As leaders, we have an obligation to be responsive, authentic, empathetic, and transparent with the people with whom we interact. If you invest in responsiveness, the reward will come in an enhanced reputation for follow-through and dependability—key foundational elements for trust and accountability.

When it comes to building a balanced workplace, responsiveness matters.

Body Language and Tone: The Other 93 Percent

When I was growing up, communication skills were primarily taught by focusing on the written or spoken word. In speech class, it was more important that the content of our presentation met with a specific rubric. We seldom, if ever, received feedback on our tone or body language beyond "stand up straight" and "slow down." Unfortunately, speech class carried such a negative stigma that we were all terrified of the experience, so the feedback probably wouldn't have gotten through anyway.

Instead of focusing on what we were saying and in what order, it may have been more important for us to focus on the *how*. In his 1971 work *Silent Messages*, Albert Mehrabian introduced the 7-38-55 rule, which hypothesized that 7 percent of communication is verbal, 38 percent is tone of voice, and 55 percent is attributable to body language.[10] We're not going to argue about the validity of the study or the precision of the percentages. However, let's agree that a large proportion of communication is nonverbal and that, in particular, we get into trouble when our spoken words don't match what our tone and bodies are saying.

I am by no means an expert in the subconscious mind, but my body—and especially my face—routinely gives me away when I'm communicating with others. As mentioned previously, I'm introverted and analytical. As such, I tend to watch intently what's going on around me and enter into a conversation only if the topic suits me or if I'm in a more familiar setting. More often than not, this behavior leaves those around me wondering what I'm thinking—they're left to fill in the blanks of my nonverbal communication. The result is that I'm frequently misunderstood and labeled as aloof, uncaring, or detached.

There are definitely times when I'm lost in my own little world, not paying attention to the vigorous conversation going on around me—but that's not the norm. Most of the time, I'm waiting until I have something meaningful to say or mustering up the courage to jump in while the extroverts effortlessly flit between story lines and talk over one another.[11] What I don't do often enough is think about how my body and face may be

---

10. *Silent Messages* by Albert Mehrabian, 1971; Wadsworth Publishing Company.

11. It drives me particularly crazy when there are multiple conversations happening at once. I have no idea how someone can keep a multithreaded conversation going *and* take anything meaningful away from the interaction.

speaking on my behalf and sending messages that my conscious mind doesn't intend to send.

As our communication tools evolve from text based to video, the other 93 percent will become of even greater importance. The etiquette around video communication is still evolving, but some basic rules around non-verbal communication still apply. The camera captures only so much, and there is always a risk that the person on the other end is distracted by something offscreen. Without being able to see a person's whole body, there is a greater opportunity to be disingenuous. I might be speaking with a colleague on one screen, but that individual might be more engaged in the video streaming on another screen or might be distracted by their phone, strategically held just out of view. Especially in meetings with more than a handful of participants and especially when those participants are working from home, the opportunity to be disingenuous over video communications is immense compared to in-person meetings.

We've all been in meetings populated with a few "tourists": colleagues who were invited so they didn't feel left out of the conversation but who don't actually have anything meaningful to contribute. In a conference room setting, tourists sit quietly and blend in with the furniture, but over video they might turn off their camera and leave the room altogether. Though there may seem to be minimal harm in tourists tuning out—literally—to a meeting where they have little to contribute, the time dedicated by tourists represents a real loss in productivity and can contribute to disengagement.

Ask the average middle manager and they will tell you that they're completely bogged down by meetings, many of which are unnecessary or uninteresting to them. Over time, those hours spent in meetings where they don't belong can lead them to believe that their contributions to the business aren't valued. I sincerely hope that the widespread adoption of video-based communication will change the culture of meetings and lead to a world where we can host meetings with only the people who really need to be there.

The point is that as our communication tools evolve from primarily text based to more video based, our body language will play a greater role in our ability to communicate effectively.

The other night, Linda and I were relaxing over a glass of wine. Our relationship is really tight at this point in our journey together, and we're having a lot of fun enjoying each other's company. We were watching a television show where the characters were discussing nonverbal communication. Linda looked at me, pursed her lips, and moved them slightly to the side. After thirty-six years of togetherness, my interpretation of this look was that of mild skepticism sprinkled with a hint of curiosity to learn more. I immediately told her of my interpretation, and she pursed harder and moved her lips even more to the side—adding a slight nose crinkle. To me, this enhanced facial expression was one of disbelief that I could possibly be correct. Sometimes a blind squirrel does find a nut!

Apparently, as I was celebrating, my left eyebrow lifted slightly and my head cocked to the right, which is my "I'm right, aren't I?" look. She immediately called me on it and nailed her assessment. After nearly four decades of living with a man of few words, she's become an expert in reading my facial expressions. Almost without fail, she knows when I'm out of sorts and is highly skilled at getting me to open up about what's gnawing at me. Earlier in our journey, this really bothered me—I didn't find it helpful to be called out, and I certainly didn't want to open up to my feelings.

(Important sidebar: If you're reading this and have a personality profile similar to mine, open your mind to this kind of help from those closest to you. If you take anything away from this book, opening up and sharing what's eating at you in a safe environment is one of the healthiest things you can do. Take it from me—keeping everything bottled up only makes matters worse.)

A basic understanding of body language can be a powerful tool in the workplace. Recently, I was in a one-on-one business meeting with "Bob" where I was making a fairly substantial ask for a project we were working on. As I was presenting the pitch, Bob was sitting opposite me with his arms folded. There was what I interpreted to be a look of curiosity on his face, so I was confident we were headed in the right direction. However, I also felt I needed to change tack to help him open up—his folded arms were sending a signal that he was "closed" to the message I was sending.

After a quick situational check, I realized that I was talking too much about me and not enough about the benefits the project would have on his personal brand and his business. Frankly, I was just talking too much. A few open-ended questions and some active listening got things back on track. By the end of the meeting, Bob and I were seeing eye to eye, and we agreed to meet again in two weeks to move the project forward.

By noticing that Bob was initially closed off, I was able to save the meeting. Please don't misinterpret—I'm no sales expert, and I'm not a trained psychologist. I'm just a guy who was mindful and applied some simple body language guidelines to produce a better result. It also demonstrates how you can elicit different responses based on your posture, tone, and demeanor, assuming the other party is paying attention.

I've also found that if I look people in the eye, I'm much less prone to being misinterpreted. Eye contact can be very uncomfortable, but it's also disarming and shows that you're engaged in the conversation. In my opinion, it helps your counterparty know that you're interested in what they have to say and are present in the moment.

Even through video communication, if the other party doesn't glance up and look directly into the camera on occasion, I might suspect that they're paying closer attention to something out of my view.

Recently, I was in a one-on-one meeting over video with someone I don't normally interact with. As the conversation progressed, I couldn't help but notice that he was completely avoiding the camera. Although his behavior was likely unintentional, it made me feel like he would have rather been somewhere else. Attendees in meetings want to feel like you care and that you're engaged. It's hard, but you can indeed "look me in the eye" over video—it just takes a bit of awareness and effort.

Trust me, making eye contact is one of the hardest things for an introvert to do—it takes training and practice. This is another area where balance is key—too little eye contact and you're labeled as "shifty," too much and you're a "creeper."

Mindfulness is also key. Actively think about how you're positioning yourself and how your face is responding to various stimuli. I won't comment on all the ways that the subconscious mind develops, but training and repetition develop your subconscious.[12] Through awareness and practice of your body positioning, you can train how your body responds in certain situations. Be aware that this training will take time, and forgive yourself if you revert to old habits in the heat of battle. As you work on these new skills, it's important to find a safe place to practice them. There are certainly seminars on the topic, but it can be fun to practice with someone you trust implicitly (spouse or significant other), and you're likely to get better feedback.

In the future, I hope that our K–12 systems make speech class a safer place to give and receive feedback. If today's experience is anything like the one

12. Example: When I taught my first class of CFA students back in 1990, I used every brain cell available. Ten years later, I could teach a three-day CFA Level II class with my eyes closed; my subconscious mind was driving the bus.

I went through, it's no wonder that a significant proportion of the population would rather swim with sharks than speak in public.[13]

In today's geographically diverse, work-from-home world, the time we spend together at retreats and off-sites is more valuable than ever to nurture and reinforce direct human connections. Because our opportunities to discuss issues directly are rare, let's all take a moment to understand how we carry ourselves and how others are likely interpreting our movements. So much is said through nonverbal communication that we must spend purposeful time developing our nonverbal voice.

After all, we're all actors in an elaborate production. We all play important roles that vary widely in work and play—father, friend, son, colleague, bandmate, civic leader, and philanthropist. It's critical that we understand how our conscious and subconscious minds approach each role so that we can be positive, contributing members of the troupe.

But, then again, maybe Bob was just cold and needed a sweater.

Johnny Got Bullied Today

The value of strong communication skills can be easily lost when they're not accompanied by emotional intelligence. A very grave situation that recently occurred in my family outlines how communication that's divorced from emotional intelligence can have dangerous outcomes, so buckle up—this might be tough for some of you to hear.

Just after the 2020 New Year, I received a phone call from my older sister. She was extremely distressed and filled me and Linda in on the events of the day.

My great nephew—we'll call him Johnny for the purpose of this story—was at middle school that day and was being bullied by the kids in one of his

---

13. Glenn Croston, "The Thing We Fear More Than Death," *Psychology Today,* November 29, 2012.

classes. Apparently, this is a fairly routine occurrence. He's small for his age and has had his share of life challenges that make him "different." In bully speak, those differences make him a target.

Not able to take the abuse any longer, Johnny abruptly got up from his chair and stormed out of the classroom. As he walked down the hall, he was confronted by two girls from another class, who asked where he was going. He replied, "I'm going to kill myself." Not thinking he was serious, they walked away, and Johnny proceeded down the hall. He headed straight for the second-story balcony, where he attempted to fulfill his wish by launching his body into the air.

Long story short, Johnny is okay. He was rushed to the hospital and was found to have limited physical injuries. He does, however, have deep emotional scars that will take years, if not a lifetime, to heal.

I'm telling you this story because it has direct applicability to our adult lives and to our success, or lack thereof, as business leaders. I've outlined the value of emotional intelligence in other sections, specifically as it relates to technological disruption and a rapidly changing workforce. After this incident, though, I feel the need to reiterate just how important these skills can be in business and in life.

When leaders say that college graduates aren't work-ready, this is what they mean. Most would agree that the outputs of our education system (new recruits) are woefully unprepared to think critically, act with empathy, communicate, and be effective team members. They might have acquired a solid base of technical skills but are unprepared emotionally.

Unfortunately, the problem goes much deeper than our colleges and universities, or even high schools. To get at the root cause of our lack of workplace readiness, we have to dial the clock way back.

I've been talking for a few years to whomever I can about the importance of feeding our young people, because a malnourished and stressed brain faces great difficulty retaining and recalling information.[14] In many school districts across the country, a large population of students receive free or reduced-price meals to help make up for a lack of food at home. To see just how widespread this is, take some time to read your local ALICE report from the United Way.[15] You'll be shocked.

The point to be made here is that our elementary schools pass underprepared learners to middle schools, which pass underprepared learners to high schools. Those who make it to college are not prepared for work at that level either. Ultimately, the buck is passed to employers, who have to clean up the mess.

Up to this point, I've been correlating the hunger and stress felt by our next generation to challenges in the home—such as broken families and absent parents. However, there's an added layer of stress that comes from their peers in the form of bullying.

To be clear, bullying is often the manifestation of broken homes and families.[16] It is the vehicle that transports the thoughts of weak, underdeveloped minds (of all ages) in a desperate attempt to help the bully feel better at the expense of individuals they deem inferior or who they don't understand—boys and girls like Johnny.

---

14. In a 2013 survey of teachers conducted by the Association for Supervision and Curriculum Development (ASCD), titled *Hungry Kids: A Solvable Crisis*, an overwhelming majority credited breakfast with increased concentration, better academic performance, and better classroom behavior. Overall, 90 percent of teachers agreed that breakfast is very important to academic achievement. Unfortunately, one in five American children live in families that struggle to put food on the table.

15. https://www.unitedforalice.org

16. In 2006, a team of researchers from University of Washington and Indiana University, led by Nerissa S. Bauer, found that violence in the home leads to higher rates of childhood bullying. Their study, *Childhood Bullying Involvement and Exposure to Intimate Partner Violence*, concluded that children who witness violence between parents are at higher risk of demonstrating violent behavior themselves.

As a society, we must address bullying and its negative effects. To do this, we can apply a three-pronged approach to improving the emotional quotient (EQ) of the average citizen.

First, businesses should double down on training efforts around empathy, team building (meaningful work, not just beanbag tossing and trust falls), emotional intelligence, and situational awareness. If we have more adults in our society acting like adults, we'll model different behaviors for our next generation. Kids have to see that it's not cool to judge and bully. College and school administrators need to hear loud and clear from business leaders that these skills are critical to creating higher-functioning employees. Let's get the demand-supply equation right.

Second, let's build emotional intelligence and other behavioral training into our school curricula at all levels. I'm not talking about "book learning" or didactic teaching but about simulations and other methods of embedding the work so we know that learning is being applied. Parents should be periodically invited into the process so they know how to support these efforts in the home, where they matter most. The recent trend to install social and emotional learning (SEL) curricula in our schools is a step in the right direction.[17]

Third, let's change our entertainment consumption patterns. Unfortunately, our modern media is flooded with examples that model the wrong behaviors. Can you say *Real Housewives of Idaho* or *Big Brother Season 97*? However salacious those train wrecks are—turn them off and tune them out. Also, social media makes it far too easy to anonymously lurk and throw stones that wouldn't be thrown if there were more transparency in communication.

Are we in danger of "turning soft"? The answer is "yes" if we solely focus on EQ without achieving the appropriate balance against accountability.

---

17. https://casel.org

As we improve societal EQ, we also need to significantly improve our ability to engage in challenging conversations to hold one another accountable in a constructive fashion. It takes real work to design proper accountability frameworks in families, schools, and businesses. It's much easier to gather by the water cooler, toss stones, hide behind social media tools, and tear others down without fear of consequence.

Adults must model bravery and candor to our next generation. Remember the two girls in the hall who heard Johnny say he was going to kill himself? I would bet that at least one of them had a pit in her stomach and thought she probably should say something. She didn't speak up, likely because it's uncomfortable and it's an unusual occurrence to see someone speak out against something that doesn't feel right.

Think about your own experience in your business. How many times have you known in your heart of hearts that something was wrong and instead of saying something, you let it slide? Or maybe you raised your voice once and got slapped down for speaking out. I've been guilty on all counts. We need to build more grit and bravery in the workplace. Silence is tacit approval for wrongdoing or unacceptable behavior.

We're all human, and humans make mistakes. What's important is that we learn and grow from our life's errors. I recall with great pain the times that I've judged inappropriately to make myself feel better at someone else's expense. I've been the bully because I thought I was cool and had the right to talk down to others.

The facts are that I likely didn't have all the facts, didn't understand what the other person was going through, and didn't expend any energy to try. In those moments, I wasn't brave; I was a coward. I lacked basic emotional intelligence skills.

You might be asking, "What can I do right now?" If the solutions mentioned above seem too big, hairy, and audacious, I've got three suggestions.

First, fine-tune your antennae and begin catching yourself in the small judgments you make every day. If you catch one or two before they leak out into the wild, that'll be progress. Over time, you'll get better at it. Others will see you modeling different behaviors, creating a virtuous cycle in your orbit.

Second, ask your employer to invest more in meaningful behavioral training. The evidence is overwhelming: Healthy companies that build trust and accountability outperform those that don't. Investing in building EQ and bravery in a corporate setting makes good business sense and will have the knock-on effect of building stronger adults and families. It's really hard to be a model citizen at work and consciously decide to be a jerk at home. One feeds the other.

Third, donate your time and money to organizations that are dedicated to building strong family units and respectful, high-functioning children and adults. The United Way, Boys and Girls Clubs of America, and YMCA are good bets. Make a meaningful contribution of your time, talent, or money.

Let's do something about bullying. Our society has become too fractured and polarized. We fight too much in ways that aren't productive or constructive. We've lost the ability to combine emotional intelligence with strong communication skills in order to demonstrate the empathy, understanding, and situational awareness that can make all the difference.

We need to do better. Johnny is counting on you.[18]

---

18. If you or someone you know is struggling with depression and suicidal thoughts, please contact the National Suicide Prevention Lifeline at 1-800-273-TALK (8255) or suicidepreventionlifeline.org.

PART 4
The Whole Self

In October of 2003, my high school's graduating class of 1978 was preparing to gather for its twenty-fifth reunion. I wasn't a member of that particular class, but my elder sister was. To mark the occasion, a friend of hers was recruiting musicians from their class to act as the entertainment for the evening.

It had been nearly twenty years since I had last performed, but I reluctantly agreed to get up on stage and sing some backing vocals. Somewhere in the middle of that event, among the lights and the sounds of the crowd, I realized that something important had been missing from my life.

To an outsider, it would appear that everything had fallen into place for me. I was a successful business leader and family man; but below the surface, things were beginning to unravel. Two months later, I walked out on my family.

Screech! Wait . . . you did what??

Yes, on Christmas Day 2003, I did the most cowardly, self-centered thing I've ever done. *Christmas Day*.

The story of how our marriage unraveled will have to wait for the next book, but suffice it to say, I was way *out of balance*. I was one-dimensional—work, work, and more work filled my life.

It was one of the most difficult periods of my life, but music (along with a lot of individual and marriage counseling) proved to be a key ingredient in my quest to find more meaning, purpose, and balance in my life.

Just so I don't leave you hanging, Linda and I did get fully divorced but found our way back to each other and repaired our family through hard work and dedication. Linda is a gracious, giving woman, and I literally owe my life to her. We're now happily remarried and stronger than ever.

Anyway, back to the story . . .

My elder sister Elizabeth was the lead singer at that pivotal twenty-fifth reunion party, but she was already a member of two other bands and couldn't commit to a third. So when the band decided to continue performing after the reunion party—and given the depths of my situation at the time—I happily volunteered to take on lead vocals and rhythm guitar.

By the time Linda and I were finding our way back to one another in mid-2005, The Remainders were performing for live audiences on a regular basis.[1] It's hard to put into words, but the pulse and drive of rock 'n' roll music was just what the doctor ordered to open my mind to the possibility that there was much more to life than spreadsheets, budgets, and performance reviews.

When a band "finds its groove," it's a magical experience. The cares of the world melt away, and you're transported into a state of nirvana. The

---

1. Check us out at https://www.facebook.com/TheRemainders.

real magic happens when the band shares its groove with an audience of willing participants, but getting to that point takes practice. Lots of practice. That is why on a typical Monday night, you can find me entering a nondescript building on the south side of La Crosse, Wisconsin, joined by five other gentlemen.

Our studio is the epitome of grunge, a real "man cave." There's a makeshift soundstage at the end of the largest room in the building, which was a creamery back in the 1920s. The lighting is a combination of Christmas light jumbles, old table lamps, and LED pucks that we'd be too embarrassed to be seen with in public. Once assembled, we usually mill about; talk about our workweek, family, travel plans, etc.; prepare our instruments; and get ready to play.

Today, the band exists for two primary purposes—the first is to engage in musical philanthropy. Nearly all of our performances are designed to give back to the community that's given so much to us over the years.

The second is to channel our artistic talents in a constructive way, providing each member with a unique, head-clearing experience. Selfishly, the second purpose is the most important. For each member, the band provides a necessary escape from the daily grind of our work lives—and we all need it. Our bassist is an otolaryngologist, our man on the keys owns a heating and A/C business, our drummer is a fourth-grade teacher, our lead guitarist is a cheesemaker, and our sax player is a retired university professor. Okay, maybe the sax player is already chill, but the rest of us need the escape!

When I step up to the microphone, every care and worry I have melts away. The music washes over me, and the process of refining and continually improving our act takes over. I explore different vocalizations, concentrate on my breathing mechanics, and commit to muscle memory how to most efficiently sing and play guitar simultaneously.[2]

For me, the band provides a key balancing mechanism in my life. After I gave up on my dream of being a rock star, I quit music altogether. I became that guy who was all work, all the time, and the results were not optimal. I convinced myself that I had to provide economic security for my family; my ego always pushed for more growth and success. Neither one of those things is necessarily bad, but when they consume you, there's no room for anything else. Ultimately, something has to give. Health, relationships, and family are the usual suspects.

In my case, it was relationships and family. I have a handful of regrets in my life, but one that nags at me periodically is the fact that I should have spent more time with my wife and sons—really engaging with them. Sure, I was "around," but I was always thinking about what was next at work. If I had really engaged, would I have ended up in a different place than I am today? Possibly. Could I have honed the skill of being more present when I was there? Absolutely.

When I'm interviewing a prospective team member, the question I always ask is: what do you do for fun outside the office? The candidate's answer can be a key tipping point for me. A lack of outside interests can signal that either (a) the candidate is not highly motivated or (b) the candidate becomes immersed in work at the expense of family and friends. If (a), then the candidate doesn't belong in our culture. If (b), a breakdown is likely to occur at some point in the future—which will be expensive for both the individual and the company.

Most important, knowing that the candidate engages in a mentally or physically challenging hobby signals to me that they have the mental agil-

---

2. This is a real achievement for me since I can't chew gum and walk at the same time! I'm also self-taught on the guitar, which adds to the challenge (formal lessons are highly recommended).

ity to take on new tasks and are able to change and grow based on the ever-shifting priorities of the business. The candidate likely has room for more than one passion in life and is not one-dimensional, as I was for many years after I gave up on music.

In my opinion, this interview question is also essential to cultivating a healthy culture. Because we're bringing our "whole selves" to work—and the risks of being out of balance are high for both the employee and the company—understanding and embracing what makes someone tick outside the office is an important element for team cohesion.

My heart sinks when I hear people say, "I can't take on a hobby. I'm not talented." What that response tells me is that at some point in the individual's life, a mentor, coach, or teacher provided negative feedback that was never overcome.

I've been guilty of providing crass or unhelpful feedback that makes me feel important or smarter in the moment but has a long-lasting impact on the recipient's ego or outlook on their capabilities. It's my job as a leader and mentor to provide truthful, constructive, and supportive feedback to those around me. It's a leader's job to build people up, not tear them down.

I believe the biggest barrier to becoming multidimensional is our always-on, hyperconnected, social media world where if you put yourself "out there," you're expected to be perfect. Brief clips of one's achievements go viral without showcasing the hours of work and dedication that preceded them. As a result, the internet has a tendency to celebrate perfection and bash everything else. If you're not perfect, internet trolls are waiting to tear you down and make you feel unworthy.

There are myriad examples of individuals who have broken down physical and mental barriers to pursue their dreams. You don't necessarily need to be the next Rob Mendez,[3] but we all have rhythm. We are all athletes. We can all pursue our passions. When we're pursuing a passion, life is more likely to be filled with constructive experiences that help us learn and grow.

When I meet multidimensional candidates, I'm more confident they will exhibit the enhanced levels of mental agility that are necessary in today's fast-paced business environment. If they've demonstrated the strength that's required to take on a new hobby—to treat early failures as learning experiences—they're likely equipped to manage the disruption and rapid adaptation that will be required in a work environment that leverages increasingly sophisticated tools like AI and big data. Being multidimensional also sends a signal that they have persisted and persevered through adversity.

Yes, the college degree is primarily a credential that signals persistence and perseverance, but it's not the only such signal that matters. To become proficient in, or reach an expert level in, a hobby or craft outside of their direct profession tells me that these individuals have reached points in their training where they've wanted to give up but pushed through to the next level of competency, and then the next, and then the next.

For example, if creating stained glass art is your thing, you likely have dozens of failed projects that were learning experiences for projects that did ultimately see the light of day. This ability to learn from mistakes and persevere in the face of adversity is definitely a trait I want team members to exhibit. If a candidate can do it for a hobby, they can absolutely do it in a business setting.

Balance is hard to achieve and needs constant attention to maintain. My ask of you is to purposefully reflect on the concepts of work/life balance

---

3. An award-winning high school football coach who was born without arms and legs. ESPN's Wayne Drehs wrote a profile on him after Mendez was awarded an ESPY in 2019, that's certainly worth a read.

and become more multidimensional. Once you determine the path forward, start small. Test the waters—take a class or talk to some experts about how they achieved their level of competency. Also, *make* the time to pursue your passion. Earlier in my career, my dear mother and I were talking about something that I wanted to do outside the office. My response was, "I don't have the time." Mother quickly responded with, "Andy, it's not that you don't *have* the time, it's that you're *not making the time.*" This subtle difference has stuck with me since—if something is a priority, you will make the time for it.

The moral of this story is that hiring multidimensional individuals who share their talents with others is a signal of mental agility, persistence, and perseverance—all traits and skills that are essential for a growth mindset. We've also reiterated the importance of being present in both work and play to maximize productivity and promote healthy relationships.

The band has been performing for sixteen years, and I consider each member to be a brother. I'm the middle child sandwiched between two sisters, so having this many brothers is a real treat for me. We respect each other, say what needs to be said, and are a true team. Although I'm the front man and leader, The Remainders is a team sport. I wouldn't be the man I am today without their partnership. Thanks, guys.

Hold On

While we're on the subject, I want to share a specific example of how music has played a significant role in my life and highlight how denying myself the joy that comes from performing held me back personally and professionally.

Recently, The Remainders nailed a song I've wanted to play in front of live audiences for decades. The progressive rock band Kansas has been a favorite of mine since I was a boy, cranking out hits like "Carry On Wayward

Son" and "Dust in the Wind." Performing these songs has given me great joy over the years.

Their song "Hold On" was written by Kerry Livgren and was released in 1980 on the *Audio-Visions* album. I fell in love with it the first time I let the vinyl spin. It's cerebral, challenging music that, up to this point in my musical journey, has taken a back seat to more upbeat, crowd-pleasing tunes.

According to a brief Wikipedia article, Mr. Livgren wrote this song to help convince his wife to convert to Christianity—something I never realized until doing research for this book.[4] Viewed through my lens, the lyrics take a more secular tone.

When I sing "Hold On," I'm reminded of the personal and professional struggles we go through as we wind our way through this wonderful gift of life we've been given. Our responsibility to that gift is to live life to the fullest and make a difference along the way. However, during the journey, we invariably lose our way. Perspectives get warped, judgment becomes clouded, and we find ourselves out of balance.

Let's break down the song by verse to illustrate how it's inspired and helped me rebalance through the years. I recommend you find the song on your favorite music service and give it a listen as you read on.

Verse 1: *Look in the mirror and tell me, just what you see . . .*

The first verse of this song has served as a reminder over the last forty years to truly look at myself in the mirror and ask myself what I see. Do I have a clear line of sight to what's important? Are my goals coherent and achievable? Have I made concessions and trade-offs I'm not proud of? Have I spoken the truth? Are my mind and heart open to change? Am I the best version of myself at this moment?

---

4. https://en.wikipedia.org/wiki/Hold_On_(Kansas_song)

This exercise of looking myself directly in the mirror has great value. When I'm looking into my own eyes, it's difficult to hide the truth or justify the questionable things I've done or said. It promotes reckoning and self-reconciliation. I almost always leave this exercise with one thing I'm going to work on in the future in an effort to continuously improve.

If you choose to engage in this practice, I recommend you only pick one thing to take action on. It's very easy to get overwhelmed and paralyzed by all the things you need to improve. Pick one so you can focus and make progress.

Verse 2: *Don't you recall what you felt when you weren't alone . . .*

The second verse helps me to be thankful for family and relationships—both professional and personal. It also serves as a reminder that self-love and self-reliance are key ingredients to happiness and success. It's a reminder that I have agency and responsibility—I'm in charge of how I feel.

While connections and friendships are to be nurtured and developed, we must be okay living in our own skin. As I look back on my life, I realize that some of my most destructive behaviors evidenced themselves when I found myself isolated and alone. In hindsight, it's obvious that I did not invest enough energy in understanding my inner self and instead clung to the notion that material goods and false adoration would fill the holes inside me. Bad things invariably happen when a heart is filled with jealousy, anger, uncertainty, and fear.

What lifts my spirit in times of loneliness and isolation is a belief in myself and the joy of helping to develop other humans. Time, experience, and hard work have helped me develop a deep sense that there's something bigger than me out there to contribute to.

Verse 3: *Let it all go and you'll know you're on the right track . . .*

I'm not a particularly religious man. I place my faith in the power of love, reason, logic, hard work, and the joy of helping others. While this verse explicitly refers to the presence of a higher being, I've always interpreted the message to mean that opportunity is at your door.

We tend not to recognize opportunity when it knocks because our minds are clouded by previous failures we didn't learn from. We don't see opportunity standing in front of us. Instead, we remain haunted by the unproductive words of a teacher, colleague, or family member who told us that our dream didn't have merit or that we couldn't do something.

To learn and grow, we must set aside all the accumulated baggage in our lives. This verse reminds me to learn and extract value from the past, but to then let it all go so I can become that next best version of myself.

Music is a powerful force for good in this world. I'm an old rock 'n' roller, but you can find meaningful, positive messages across genres and generations. I encourage you to find peace, solace, wisdom, and energy within the music that resonates with you.

The Rise of Individuality in the Workplace

One of the most deep-seated instincts is to band together and cooperate to ensure survival.

This instinct carries through to the modern corporation. We follow persuasive leaders who help us open our minds to create new products and new markets. We form teams that specialize around function and skill in an attempt to optimize for scale, service, and profitability. However, these are the same teams and specialized roles that can lead to soul-crushing conformity and repetition.

One key difference between today's workplace and the workplace of the 1990s is that individuals are bringing more of their "whole selves" to work. The lines between work and play are blurring, and we have an increasingly remote and socially connected workforce.

I believe strongly that our ability to actively listen and *be present* is a key element to striking an appropriate work/life balance. If we're constantly distracted at work or play, are we really ever spending quality time with anyone or giving anything our full attention? I still feel fractured and fragmented—being present is the number one thing I'm working on today. I'm confident that if I continually improve in this regard, the return on investment for this skill will be high at work, at play, and at home.

Looking back on the early days of my career, I realize that I hired people who I thought would be likely to conform to my way of thinking. My ego and relative lack of experience (and confidence) led me to hire team members who were less likely to challenge me and more likely to fall in line. This was not a conscious behavior on my part but was a common mistake that resulted in uniformity at the expense of balance. In retrospect, I can see that although we moved fast as a team, with more diversity of thought and opinion we would likely have been much further along on our journey.

For too long, leaders have modeled their teams in their own image, failing to appreciate the value of diverse and varied perspectives. According to a 2018 study by the Boston Consulting Group,[5] companies with *below*-average diversity scores reported a 26 percent annual boost in revenue from innovation, while those with *above*-average diversity scores reported a 45 percent increase in innovation revenue. Overall, teams with higher diversity scores enjoyed 19 percent greater overall revenue, and it serves to reason.

---

5. Rocío Lorenzo, Nicole Voigt, Miki Tsusaka, Matt Krentz, and Katie Abouzahr, *How Diverse Leadership Teams Boost Innovation*, January 23, 2018; Boston Consulting Group.

Companies don't exist in a vacuum. They need to create products and services for a highly diverse marketplace and also work alongside a diverse array of partners, vendors, and suppliers. Those companies that are too monolithic will often miss opportunities that don't resonate with their customers' unique life experiences and will struggle to maintain business relationships with those that don't see the world through a similar lens. When teams are more diverse, they are much better equipped to spot opportunities and potential problems that fall into others' blind spots.

Moving forward, one of the most difficult tasks of a manager will be to embrace the personalities of individual team members and to provide the space necessary for free expression and creativity. The reason this is so difficult is the strong countervailing pressures of on-time delivery and goal achievement. It won't be enough to loosen the dress code or encourage folks to wear goofy socks.

The leader of the future will need to encourage constructive conflict, understand how to effectively resolve discord, improve their listening skills, and show the appropriate level of personal vulnerability. This last point is key: team members won't bring their "whole selves" to help solve challenges if the boss is suited up in impenetrable armor.

The average employee of the future will need to develop much more attuned situational awareness and emotional intelligence (EQ) antennae to understand the right time to let their creativity and individuality shine. Those same antennae will need to effectively interpret signals that show when it's time to fall in line and support the team.

I believe our high school and college curricula should be altered to ensure that students are nurturing their EQ, practicing situational awareness, building creativity muscles, and learning what it means to be a great follower—all in the appropriate proportions.

Note that the preceding recommendation contains actions and encourages embedding these skills through application and practice. Demonstrating proficiency via a multiple-choice test won't cut it.

The miracle of life is that we organize. The miracle of the human condition is that we balance our innate individuality with the need to cooperate. We work together pragmatically to achieve common aims. We've learned through millennia to set aside our individuality and join with a group to develop and grow. An African proverb applies here, "If you want to go fast, go alone. If you want to go far, go together." I would adjust the proverb to say, "If you want to go fast, go with a monochromatic team. If you want to go far, go with a team filled with diversity of backgrounds, perspectives, and ideas."

I've made some decent strides in this area over the last few years—hiring team members from different backgrounds with different perspectives—but I have to do more. The hardest thing is to let their lights shine and reach consensus to move forward with agility and purpose.

Now, where are my Albert Einstein socks??

Words I Live By

It took me a long time to come to the realization that there can be minimal separation between the person I am at work and the person I am elsewhere. For generations, we have talked about the two facets of our lives as completely separate entities. However, if you believe one doesn't affect the other, you're likely headed for disaster, as I was during the earlier part of my career.

That is why, when I discuss my philosophy for balanced work, I'm really discussing a philosophy for a balanced life, of which work is one aspect. The words I choose to live by are not specific to one arena or the other.

It's important to note that the list of words I live by has changed over the years. It's not like I sat down when I was sixteen and said, "Here are the words that will help guide my behavior over the next forty years." The words I rely on have changed with the times and circumstances of my life. For me, it's important to periodically reevaluate the path I'm on and determine if a course correction is needed.

Today, I've got six words that I use as a guide to my interactions with other humans and to how I approach solving the challenges I face. When I get into a difficult situation, whether at work or at home, I pull out the list. Then I pick one or two that apply to whatever I'm dealing with, take a few centering breaths, and think about how I can turn those words into action to move forward.

Calm

In all the leadership roles I've held, the first word on the list has been the most important—*calm*.

When the stress rises, I try to be a calming influence to those around me. Being all "spun up" and anxious about a situation rarely helps. If I'm nervous, folks around me also get anxious, and we spin in a negative cycle. It's damn near impossible to influence positively and effectively when the team is distracted by unnecessary stress. The way out is to strive to be calm.

The key to remaining calm is to continually grow and learn as a human. If you're a knowledge seeker, the unknown becomes much less scary. Over time, you develop an arsenal of solutions for challenging situations and gain confidence that no matter how thorny the problem, a solution can be found.

Sometimes, my calm demeanor can be misinterpreted to imply I don't care or I lack passion. However, a keen desire to win and make a difference lives deep inside me. I want to beat my competition, be a supportive and understanding boss, and strive to help others achieve their goals through empowerment.

I've found that showing passion and the desire to win by running around with my hair on fire is unproductive. Every now and then it's necessary, but most often I have a determined look in my eye, remain calm, and fight like hell.

Consistent

Outside the office, I'm a musician and have a heavy creative vein that runs through me. I've learned the hard way that playing things by ear (pun intended) is not an effective way to run a business.

My team and the rest of the business need me to show up consistently, day in, day out. Erratic behavior or uncertainty in communication or planning typically result in team members who fill in the blanks with their own interpretations. If you've ever played the telephone game, you know how easy it is for a message to become garbled as it passes down the line without consistent reinforcement.

Working from my foundation of creativity and introversion, it can be difficult for me to remain consistent. My subconscious wants to flit from shiny ball to shiny ball and expects everyone else to be executing their tasks without question. My conscious mind knows that my erratic core doesn't lead to good business results.

That's why I'm on a personal continuous improvement (CI) journey and have introduced the concept into our company's vernacular—to strike the optimal balance between creativity and consistency.

Persistent

There have been many times throughout my career when I've faced headwinds or encountered obstacles to a cause, initiative, or job I believe in. A little voice lives inside all of us that whispers, "The easy way is to give up." That voice can take many forms, including, "No one cares anyway, so why should I?"

I've listened to that voice on occasion, and I'm almost always disappointed I did. Nothing is free, and there are very few things that are easy. It takes grit to succeed. If you believe in something and want to make a difference, persistence is important. Having hobbies and interests outside of work can help build persistence. If I had listened to that little voice that told me I wasn't good enough, I would have never picked back up the guitar or stepped up to the microphone, and an important element of my life would be missing.

A big part of persistence and grit is knowing when to adjust your position and approach a challenge from a new angle. Persistence does not mean beating your head against the same wall until you're bleeding; persistence requires keen situational awareness to pivot when appropriate. My first foray into music wasn't successful, and it took decades to find an approach that would allow me to perform in front of live audiences again.

This need to pivot has led some to accuse me of being, at times, inconsistent. I don't doubt that I've shown inconsistent behavior over the years. Many times, though, I'm simply repositioning to improve the odds that the organization meet a long-term goal.

On a related note, please allow me to step back on my soapbox. It drives me crazy when I see adults/parents wearing "I Can't Adult Today" shirts—just think about the indirect signal that's being sent to their children about lessons in persistence and grit. It's our responsibility as adults to model positive behaviors. Thanks for listening, I feel better . . .

Thoughtful

Of the words I live by, *thoughtful* is the hardest for me to consistently apply in practice.

I'm an idea guy with a strong "voice" (DiSC C/D personality type). I easily get caught up in the excitement of new plans and different ways a challenge can be solved. It's easy to fall into the mental trap that my ideas are the best and that everyone around me should love them too. That trap is particularly acute due to my senior-level position, as team members can be reticent to challenge me.

I must continually remind myself that everyone I speak to has a different perspective and is dealing with their own s*** personally and professionally. Fancy psychological terminology like *situational awareness* and *emotional intelligence* is typically used in learning and development settings. However, considering the lens through which others view the world has helped me put those concepts into practice.

Being calm and thoughtful can be a double-edged sword. Some people I work with misinterpret this behavior and label me as a potential doormat. I have learned to pick my battles over the years, and when it's an issue I really care about, I'm no doormat.

Back on my soapbox for a moment. One other thing that drives me nuts is when rude people apply armchair psychology to justify their behavior. The phrase I hear the most is, "You're in control of your own feelings; no one can make you feel a certain way." While technically true, people who don't exercise thoughtfulness and instead use words to tear others down can certainly exacerbate feelings. Although I'd like to think so, people are not made of Teflon, and my lack of thoughtfulness can absolutely turn a good day into a bad one for a colleague or a friend. Back off the soapbox.

Agile

Individuals who aspire to be leaders should evaluate their willingness and ability to be mentally agile. As you climb the leadership ladder, the need to switch gears throughout the day increases substantially.

During his high school years, our son Brandon was a scratch golfer. In addition to his physical abilities, I attribute his success to his ability to reset mentally after each shot. Good shots created momentum for more good shots, and bad shots were treated as opportunities to refocus and get back on track.

I've used this mental model at work to help me reset my mental frame as I move from topic to topic throughout the day. If I allow the challenges from a prior meeting to cloud my judgment as I walk into the next meeting, I won't be bringing my best self to team members who are counting on me. I know that the agility Brandon built as a golfer is paying dividends now that he's a physician.

I find many people in business bristle at the concept of agility. I hear it all the time, "Let's do things one at a time. Let's get 'done' and move to the next project." I like "checking the box" and completing tasks just as much as the next person—I love the feeling I get when the garage is neat and tidy. In business, the concept of "done" can be elusive and difficult to define—especially for leaders.

Industrious

My Uncle Linse was a significant influence in my life—he introduced me to ice fishing, taught me how to rip apart a small engine, and gave me my first beer. To be clear, I really dislike ice fishing, but how would I have known for sure if Linse hadn't exposed me to it?

Most important, Linse showed me what it meant to be industrious. Linse was always up to something and seemed to have boundless energy. If he wasn't rebuilding the lawn mower engine in the garage, he was building a model airplane or helping a neighbor. There didn't seem to be a problem he couldn't solve. Linse and my dad both taught me that research, persistence, and logic were the tools needed to overcome a challenge and develop the most elegant solution.

As my mentor Carl Schweser told me early in my career, "Andy, if you're not moving forward, you're standing still. Not much happens when you're stationary." The saying is simple but profound. Opportunity isn't going to find you. Opportunity is sought after and found—typically through falling down and getting back up. Opportunity can be elusive but typically presents itself to the industrious, who are always learning and trying new things.

People come in all shapes and sizes—mentally and physically. I enjoy the process of identifying and writing about the words I live by and periodically reevaluate the list for relevance and effectiveness as the stages of my life ebb and flow. I highly recommend the exercise to you.

Finding the Courage to Be Vulnerable

On November 22, 1999, Carl Schweser and I sold the Schweser Study Program to Kaplan, Inc. There was tremendous change occurring in the education space at the time—primarily resulting from the advent of online delivery—and we knew that partnering with Kaplan was the right thing to do to keep pace with this rapidly changing landscape.

During the first few years with Kaplan, we drove tremendous growth in revenue and the team grew quickly. We were afforded a great deal of autonomy and flexibility to expand and transform the business into the digital sphere. It was also my first experience with financial reporting in a publicly traded company. As you might imagine, reporting growth in revenue and operating profit was easy. Good news is very straightforward to communicate.

It wasn't until around 2005 that we experienced our first "tough sledding." Enrollments at CFA Institute, the governing body for the CFA Exams, had declined slightly, and the Institute began self-publishing textbooks and other study materials—directly moving into competition with prep providers.

At the time, the headquarters of Kaplan Professional was located in Chicago, and our part of the business was located in La Crosse, Wisconsin—about a five-hour drive, depending on traffic into the city. I distinctly remember the drive from La Crosse to Chicago for my quarterly business review. I had made the trip many times before, but this was the first time that I had to report what I felt was bad news. I can't say I was afraid, but my stomach was certainly in knots—I was dreading the meeting and running through scenarios in my mind of how it would go.

Looking back, the meeting in Chicago went well. My supervisor understood the challenges and had confidence we were running the business well. Tough questions certainly had to be addressed. We had work to do, but I was also confident we were driving excellence in outcomes for our clients and students based on then-current standards for exam-training delivery. The support of my boss and his "can-do, work together to solve challenges" approach gave me confidence that the world wasn't going to end if I had bad news to share. That one experience helped me build the courage I would need later in my career to be transparent and forthcoming about both good news and bad.

I believe courage is essential; you have to be clear when communicating results both vertically and horizontally in the business. Sugarcoating doesn't help anyone in the long run. I'm not talking about the courage to run into a burning building, confront a criminal, or fight in a battle. I'm talking about the courage to stand up for what's right, engage in a challenging conversation, and strike the right balance between vulnerability and ego.

Speaking from personal experience, getting this balance right is really hard. Too much vulnerability and you're labeled a pushover; folks will take advantage of you. Too much ego and you're labeled as unapproachable and aloof; team members won't want to work with you.

Here are a few examples of how I've seen things go sideways in an organization and how exercising a little courage can help.

1. Delay

Have you ever been in an email conversation with a colleague where things are going really well? Then, in a separate email, you ask a difficult question and the individual "goes dark"? The person doesn't respond for days or maybe never responds. Although it's theoretically possible the individual missed your email, it's more likely that your colleague either doesn't know the answer, doesn't want to engage because he or she might look bad, or is trying to figure out how not to expose a weakness in part of the organization or in another colleague. I've already described how responsiveness can make a huge difference and how avoiding difficult conversations can be detrimental to team cohesion.

I've certainly been guilty of this behavior in the past and am actively working on finding the balance between vulnerability and ego so I can say, "I don't know the answer to your question, but I'll get back to you by Tuesday." I'm also working on having the courage to hold colleagues accountable for delivering what they said they would in a timely manner.

2. Hiding and Obfuscation

Two years ago, I was at a conference with a team member, and we met with a potential vendor whose product could have made a significant impact on the business. After the meeting, we discussed integrating this product into our workflow, and I was assured by the team member that he would drive the research and implementation. During reviews, I would ask about his progress in working with this vendor and would get innocuous responses like, "The team is working on it," "Our next meeting with them is in two weeks," or "The company's rep left the firm so we have to start over." After this individual left the company, to my surprise (maybe it shouldn't have been a surprise), I found that *nothing* had been done with the vendor.

In retrospect, I should have been more persistent and required a project plan and evidence of progress; this would have uncovered the passive-aggressive behavior of my team member. This individual lacked the courage to engage in constructive conflict to reach a mutually agreeable solution. Instead, to get his way, he chose to ignore the work. A simple, somewhat uncomfortable fifteen-minute conversation could have saved so much angst on both sides.

When working with numbers, hiding is an even bigger problem. I'm sure you've heard the phrase "the numbers don't lie." This means that in time, all results are revealed—either directly or indirectly. Therefore, it's much better to muster the courage to discuss negative financial or data trends early than to hide or obfuscate results. The trust erosion that ensues is difficult, if not impossible, to recover from. Waiting for results to improve to avoid a difficult conversation seldom pays off.

3. It's None of Your Business

Silos and protectionism within an organization limit growth and can potentially destroy corporate value. As discussed previously, when leaders gain more responsibility, egos tend to inflate and vulnerability decreases, and this combination can lead to turf protection. I have definitely been guilty of this behavior in the past, and now I actively work on achieving balance between ego and vulnerability—especially as it relates to transparency into what my business unit is doing.

The behavior that is particularly detrimental is the leadership view that "this is my business, and we'll share information with you on a need-to-know basis." When an organization is small, transparency is easier because communication is more straightforward and reporting lines tend to be flatter. In large organizations, lines of communication are more complex, and fiefdoms are built across product, geography, and channel. The conundrum is that as an organization grows, the benefits of sharing and collaboration increase (because there's typically more to share). Simultaneously, protectionism and silos develop as organizational lines are drawn and the number of units and reporting levels grow.

The point I'm driving at here is that the balance between ego and vulnerability can get seriously out of whack as a company grows. Leaders should be actively thinking about how to keep these two forces balanced. Leaders should have the courage to be vulnerable and invite others into their part of the company to collaborate, share, and align. I've literally been told, "It's none of your business," when I've asked to learn more about a capability that might be deployed in a different part of the organization to help another team succeed. When you're told to mind your own business, trust erodes and walls go up even higher.

All of the above depends on the culture you nurture as a leader. If you're leading by example by being firm and decisive, open and approachable, bringing your whole self to work and being vulnerable when appropriate, then you're likely creating an environment that allows team members to exhibit courage and engage in more meaningful conversations. If you shut discourse down, yell at subordinates, or are not open to new ideas, well, best of luck.

While we can all aspire to be courageous in the workplace, the average human only has so much capacity for conflict, likely suffers from some type of public-speaking anxiety,[6] and can rapidly become disenchanted by toxic coworkers or cultural environments. After numerous attempts at being courageous with no feedback, compromise, or results, most employees will go looking for greener pastures. Many might use the phrase, "Life's too short."

Remember that courage is a highly personalized experience, and interpretation varies widely. What is courageous to one coworker could be viewed as standard operating procedure through the lens of another.

Courage is probably one of the most difficult concepts in business. Reporting bad news is never fun, but it's a necessary component of any leader's standard work. However much we'd all like the world to be rainbows and puppy dogs 24/7, that's not real life. Being courageous enough to report bad news along with the good gives a much clearer picture of the actual current state of the business and allows for more productive problem solving and planning to occur.

I'd recommend you spend some time reflecting on the concept of courage in the workplace and self-assessing how balanced you are as a leader on the ego-vulnerability spectrum. I'll be doing the same, and if you think I'm

---

6. Glassophobia, or the fear of public speaking, affects 73 percent of the population, according to The National Institute of Mental Health. It can take real courage and a lot of effort to mitigate this anxiety. Have you ever been talking to someone in a difficult conversation and their neck turns red and splotchy? This is likely the physical manifestation of anxiety they are experiencing in that moment. It's part of your job as a leader to be attuned to nonverbal cues and react/adjust accordingly.

out of balance, I would appreciate it if you'd let me know in a constructive manner. That's what personal continuous improvement is all about.

Grace, Dignity, and Compassion

I've already shared the six words that I live by, but since late 2008, I've relied on three more to help shape my interactions with strangers, friends, colleagues, clients, and family members. Those words are *grace*, *dignity*, and *compassion*. They served me well as we navigated the turbulent waters of the Great Recession and are proving to be particularly important during the current state of social unrest and economic upheaval.

I'd like to take a few moments to explain why these words are so important to me, and ask that we all adopt a similar construct to tamp down the seemingly meteoric rise in divisive, demeaning, polarizing, and, in some cases, dehumanizing language we routinely see deployed in our society.

I fear that we are becoming anesthetized to what would be considered vicious, uncivil, unacceptable, and unproductive discourse to a prudent observer.

Grace: *"The quality or state of being considerate or thoughtful."*[7]

This definition is clear and needs no interpretation other than what your mother or father taught you, "Treat others as you would like others to treat you." This is the Golden Rule that is found nearly universally across philosophical disciplines and religious orders. Let's take the Golden Rule seriously.

---

7.   All three definitions courtesy of https://www.merriam-webster.com.

Dignity: *"The quality or state of being worthy, honored, or esteemed."*

I apply this word both internally and externally. Certainly, I want to carry myself in a manner that exudes worth and esteem. More important, though, I want others to feel like I hold them in the same regard. We will make greater progress in creating a more diverse, inclusive, and tolerant society if we hold others in the same esteem that we hold ourselves. There are countless historical examples of what happens when we dehumanize populations or believe we're better than someone else. Almost invariably, really bad things happen when there are perceived differences in worth across populations. We should all study and learn from these examples.

Compassion: *"Sympathetic consciousness of others' distress together with a desire to alleviate it."*

Empathy and compassion are related concepts, but the latter is the stronger of the two in that compassion encompasses the ability to understand another human's pain and the desire to help. Personally, I turn that desire to help into philanthropic activities pointed primarily at education and hunger-related causes. You don't have to be wealthy to give back. Time and talent are equally important currencies for most worthy causes.

I must speak up. I must make my voice heard. Am I perfect? No—not by a long shot. Do I strive to continuously improve? Yes. Mistakes are an opportunity for reflection and growth. Yesterday, I made one of those mistakes and am thinking today about how I could have done things differently and how I can be a better version of myself in the future.

This is not a political statement; it is a plea for rational, logical, and productive public and private debate of all kinds. Caustic, divisive, and purposefully denigrating rhetoric is wildly unproductive and has no place in our society.

Changing how we speak to one another and opening our minds and hearts to the consideration of other points of view will help us move forward. We will make greater progress, enjoy more economic success, and be the shining stars on the global stage we deserve to be if we change our tack.

It's excruciatingly clear to me that our current polarized way of working is not yielding the results we've hoped for and is making the American Dream less attainable for us all. Let's strive to use more grace, dignity, and compassion as we work to keep that dream alive.

The Whole Self Superpower

If you're keeping track, I use a total of nine words to help me achieve balance at work and play. I must continually remind myself that words are just words unless they're also accompanied by deeds.

While each word has power of its own, the real strength lies in combining them. It's like a band of children's television show characters, be it the Ninja Turtles, Power Rangers, or Transformers. Each character possesses a unique power, but when combined, the group as a whole can access additional tools for thwarting their enemies. It's important to note that this set of words is *unique to me*. It's highly unlikely that you would choose the same words to help define how you interact with other humans, fight workplace disillusionment, and drive personal and professional productivity. Even if you did end up with the same set of words to live by, the emphasis placed on one trait or another would definitely differ. Just as your lens is *one size fits you*, so too are the words you choose and the emphasis you give them in any given moment.

The words you choose should hold real value and meaning in your lived experiences. In a healthy, balanced workplace, you should be encouraged to draw strength from your chosen words *and* continuously explore how your personal values interact with and augment the company's shared values. For too long, leaders valued uniformity, hired staff that shared their singular point of view, and inadvertently (or perhaps not) made those who didn't fit into the culture feel like they were playing a part that didn't suit them. That is not to suggest that shared corporate values shouldn't be promoted; leaders should strive to promote balance between the values that dictate their corporate culture and those of the individual.

The best theatrical performances are achieved by actors who are able to step into character *and* offer a genuine representation of some part of their true selves to the audience. Similarly, managers and leaders get the best performance out of themselves and their teams when they encourage bringing the whole self into the workplace. As an avid theatergoer, I can tell you that it's easy to spot when a role has been miscast and the actor is struggling to play a part that they can't relate to on a personal level. The same is true of the workplace.

When someone is made to feel like they need to conform to a role that is uncomfortable or disingenuous to them, they begin to disconnect and view the job as a means to an end. Employees who are "punching the clock" and watching it intently until the workday ends aren't expending discretionary energy to benefit their performance. While miscast actors only have to grind through an unnatural part until the show runs its course, team members who feel the need to change some part of who they are when they arrive at work will struggle with the discomfort of "performing" for eight hours a day, five days a week.

I don't fully agree with the old adage that says, "Do something you love and you'll never work a day in your life," because even those who follow their passions will have to face interpersonal and structural challenges along the way.[8] If I could rewrite this cliché, I'd say, "Find work in a field that sparks curiosity deep inside you, bring your whole self to that work, and continuously develop a balanced set of human and technical skills

---

8.   As I learned the hard way after I dropped out of school to follow my dream of becoming a rock star.

throughout your life." It's not very catchy, but this is a big part of the formula for finding joy in life and work.

When staff feel not only accepted but also appreciated as the unique and complicated people that they are, they're much more likely to find satisfaction in their roles, expend discretionary energy, and be less likely to feel hindered by the soul-crushing weight of playing a part that doesn't suit them.

I want to caution that I'm not asking people to walk into work each day and tell everybody every gory detail of their life.[9] Your private life is still your private life, but we need to recognize that what happens outside of work cannot be completely divorced from the person you are in the office. The battle scars collected through life's challenges, and the lessons learned from them, are part of the whole self that walks through the door each morning. We should be encouraged to learn from *all* aspects and versions of ourselves—our accomplishments and our failures—and recognize how that development and growth impacts the person we are in the workplace. Our experiences ultimately empower our productivity, help us relate to and collaborate with others, and open our minds to change and growth.

Whatever traumatic or difficult experiences you've had in your life—a divorce, a miscarriage, the death of a loved one—those events form part of who you are today. Pretending they never happened—playing a role that isn't true to your lived experiences—often proves more exhausting than facing those issues head-on, accepting that they are part of who you are, and learning from the scars they've left behind.

This is yet another reason why the concept of vulnerability and ego, especially within the leadership ranks, is so important. If leaders take the atti-

---

9. I know I'm being a bit of a hypocrite, airing some of my dirty laundry here, but it's only to demonstrate how my battle wounds have made me the leader I am today.

tude that demonstrating vulnerability to their staff is a weakness, others will follow their lead and feel afraid to be their true selves. They'll think twice before adding their unique perspective to the conversation, and the well-documented advantages that come from having a diversity of thought and experience will not be realized. At the same time, we need to keep in mind the importance of balance; being too emotional and vulnerable can be equally problematic.

As a leader, you want to be seen as a human being who makes mistakes so that those around you don't feel like failure is unacceptable and thus behave in an unnatural way in order to meet an impossible expectation. On the flip side, you don't want to demonstrate so much vulnerability that the workplace breaks down when a team member experiences a minor problem or creates unnecessary drama as a result of oversharing. Leaders must balance being a direct, strong, and confident leader with the ability to open up enough so that people know that it's okay to fall down, because you've fallen too and will do your best to help them back up.

Your people need to feel comfortable bringing their whole selves to work, saying what needs to be said when it needs to be said, and feeling that they're being listened to with an open, agile mind. In an environment built on trust and openness, courage and bravery are able to rise to the surface, and leaders are then able to develop and nurture talent in a more productive way.

It's important to stress that balance is a journey, not a destination. It's a North Star to continually navigate toward as circumstances shift and evolve. In recent years, I've taken up yoga and pilates. While I can find balance in complicated poses, an aching muscle or a minor distraction in the corner of my eye can throw me off. This serves as a stark reminder that moments of true balance are always fleeting; it's only a matter of time before something takes you out of that state.

Don't let unbalanced moments discourage you from continually pursuing a more balanced existence. The fact is that engaging in a journey of lifelong learning and exploration means that you *will be* thrown out of balance periodically as you move forward. *Learning requires that you become purposefully uncomfortable and work toward integrating newfound knowledge into your whole self.*

The nine words I've introduced here have served as a North Star on my journey toward striking a better balance at work and in my personal life. When combined, they have helped me to create better-performing teams and organizations, a better working environment, and a more resilient workforce. But again, words are just words, and those words are of little value until they're put into action.

Alignment

When I was fourteen years old, my dad took several 1960s-era VW Bug chassis and a few Bug engines and used them to build a "kit car" known as a Bradley GT. She was a beauty—Plexiglas gull-wing doors, headlights that automatically popped up from their resting positions flush with the body, white leather seats, and a brilliant, sparkling blue fiberglass body.

We spent long hours together on weekends and weeknights stealing parts from this chassis or that engine to put the mechanicals together and assemble the body. It was a great bonding experience that I'll never forget. Needless to say, I learned a lot from my dad about mechanical systems—how to bleed brake lines, what a carburetor does, and how to install new piston rings.

As you might expect, my primary job in the venture was to hand him the right tool at the right time, fetch parts, read him instructions, and provide moral support. I developed an intimate knowledge of the roles that specific tools played in the process and gained a keen appreciation for reading and understanding written instructions. Most of the instructions were well written and understandable, but we had the occasional challenge where we had to scratch our heads. My dad let out a few "choice words" when the instructions were written out of order or weren't clear. There were definitely more than a handful of times when we had extra parts we didn't know what to do with or were missing key pieces. By nature, I'm not the most fastidious or process-oriented guy, but this project taught me a great deal about the value of effective flow and process.

A few times during the project, Dad would let me go it alone to put together a component or two, and for the most part, I did pretty well. I had taken a small engine–repair class earlier that year in school and successfully ripped apart a lawn mower engine and put it back together. I passed the class by pulling the ripcord on the engine, and to my delight (and relief), the engine sprung to life.

One day, I was working on the car on my own and found myself missing a bolt that was supposed to fit into a nut that helped hold the body to the chassis. I searched the garage for a replacement and found a bolt that appeared to be exactly the right size to complete the task. With one turn of the ratchet, the bolt and nut fit together. The next turn was also successful—what could go wrong? I kept turning the ratchet and started to get concerned because the bolt was nowhere near all the way in, but it was getting increasingly difficult to turn. It got to the point where the bolt was completely fused with the nut, but the bolt head was still a good inch above where it was supposed to be seated.

You might be wondering why I didn't stop turning the ratchet the second I knew it wasn't going to fit. My only response is that I'm confident my frontal lobe didn't fully mature until age forty-two, and it certainly wasn't in great shape at age fourteen . . .

When Dad returned home from whatever regional accreditation visit he was on that week, I explained what I had done. As you've probably already guessed, a few choice words were spoken at full volume before the teaching began. It turns out that although the nut and bolt looked like they were the same size, one was metric and the other was imperial. Needless to say, I learned my lesson and haven't made that mistake since.

This story contains several lessons for business that apply to continuous improvement and organizational health, but the one I'd like to focus on is the value of standardization and alignment for success in collaboration. Most business leaders (myself included) espouse the value of teamwork and collaboration across departments, product lines, and divisions. Most business leaders (myself included) are also frequently disappointed by the lack of success in most collaboration efforts. In my experience, the most common reasons for collaboration failure are the lack of standardization in process, procedure, and data, as well as a misalignment of goals and incentives across teams.

Even when two teams get together with the best of intentions and (a) identify an opportunity for efficiency gains or growth, (b) properly scope the opportunity, and (c) design an effective project plan, collaboration begins to fail during implementation. Failure occurs due to the lack of standardized tools and information. This is especially acute for cross-divisional collaborations where disparate accounting systems, workflows, data storage/tagging, and cultures have been calcified over time.

In addition, the "people fit" is essential. If the team reaching out to collaborate doesn't have a willing partner on the other side, the effort is doomed from the start. While this can be attributable to egos and the tribal nature of nuclear teams, more likely than not, cross-divisional and cross-departmental goals aren't adequately aligned. When goals are aligned to a common vision, collaboration becomes more natural, and there is a clearer line of sight to the benefits of the joint opportunity. When goals are misaligned, team members begin to think the other department or division is "out to get them" by not cooperating. However, the more likely reason for a faulty collaboration is that the receiving team's goals don't fit with those of the requesting team.

The companies of the future that will win in the market, at scale, will be those that have adopted common tools and processes for similar workflows; developed common systems for tagging, storing, and interpreting their troves of data; and aligned their market-differentiating goals down, through, and across the organization.

And yes, when I turned sixteen, my father was very kind and let me drive the car. Big mistake. I summarily drove our Bradley GT into the ground over the next few years. I treated the car so badly that the steering wheel came off in my hands while I was doing thirty miles per hour down Losey Boulevard. Sorry, Dad.

Trust Is the Bedrock of Business Performance

One evening, my wife, Linda, and I were winding down after a long day. We were snuggled up on the couch watching television, and she fell asleep in my arms. During that moment of tenderness, I tuned my mind to the pattern of her breathing and tried to match my rhythm to hers. At first, keeping time was comfortable and felt natural, but after a minute or so, it became much more difficult.

In that moment, I was struck by how incredibly unique we all are. Linda and I share an extraordinary connection, but our hearts beat as one only for brief periods of time. We can see the same thing and interpret what we're looking at in different ways. We can hear the same song, but our emotional experience with the music will differ. Moments of unforced alignment are rare—even for the most in-tune couple. Full conformance is the exception; individuality is the norm.

As my thoughts continued to drift, I started to ponder individuality in the workplace. I know, you're saying, "How romantic, Andy!"

Remember, she was asleep . . .

Anyway, I thought to myself: If it's difficult for me to maintain a breathing rhythm with my soul mate, the level of difficulty maintaining alignment in a team environment must rise exponentially. It's no wonder that individuals suffocate under the weight of leaders who demand or require high degrees of conformance. As discussed previously, people are less likely to leave a company—*most leave their boss.*

Thus far, I've shared some thoughts on effective communication, on striving for balance, on bringing the whole self to work, and on the value of education and lifelong learning. All of these ingredients are necessary for creating organizational clarity, ensuring that roles are well-defined, and seeing that individuals feel empowered to share their unique perspectives. These ingredients foster healthy and productive teams that minimize internal conflict and maximize the organization's ability to perform at its highest potential. Without trust and alignment across the organization, however, all of these worthy efforts could ultimately fail to produce results.

I often hear individuals yearning for a time when their company was small. They openly complain about how complicated things have become and are nostalgic for the days when only a handful of people were working in concert. In those days of yore, communication was seamless, everybody knew what everyone else was supposed to be doing, and team members demonstrated grit, bravery, and a true commitment to getting things done, not for themselves but for the betterment of the organization. I'm being purposefully semi-sarcastic because the reality of the "days of yore" seldom meets with our cloudy, romantic memories of the past.

Unfortunately, most organizations that are successful in those early phases eventually reach a tipping point in organizational growth. As the company grows, battle lines are drawn between departments, and infighting inevitably follows. With additional hands on deck, employees feel like responsibilities that once fell solely to them are being "taken away" and delegated to others. Their base instincts lead them to believe they're under threat. Some develop a protectionist mindset, resist change, and struggle to draw a straight line between their individual contributions and the success of the organization as a whole.

In a small organization with just a few highly engaged colleagues, it can be easier to establish trust because you're in the trenches with them day in, day out. You're more likely to know what makes your work partners tick, how to get the best from them, and what their motivational triggers are. In such an environment, it can be more natural to bring your whole self to work, have challenging but necessary conversations, align around common goals, and trust that those around you have the best of intentions.

In the early 1990s, our small business—the Schweser Study Program for the CFA Exams—was successful in its early stages of growth because we trusted one another implicitly. From that trust came a natural ability to communicate, develop an effective division of labor, and work as a team. Trust was the initial condition, and we held each other accountable for our commitments. This last point is key: we must always balance trust with awareness and accountability.

After Kaplan acquired Schweser in late 1999, the organization I managed grew. It became clear that my technical expertise and limited behavioral knowledge could only take us so far. I was left routinely scratching my head, wondering why perfectly logical and well-developed plans would fail. My naïve operating assumption was that everyone trusted each other and was motivated to perform well in their jobs. After all, each team member's paycheck came from the same place, and that check was reliant on the success of the business; so why would anyone want to see colleagues or teams fail? Had I opened my mind to the importance of organizational health and continuous improvement sooner, just imagine how much better we'd be today. How many of those failed projects would have been successes instead?

To illustrate the point a different way, when we're driving an automobile down the road, we subconsciously apply an interesting combination of trust and awareness. However, the baseline assumption is that the guy next to you isn't going to drive you off the road. Oddly, in business, trust is typically not the baseline assumption of team members. Far too often, *mistrust* is the initial condition.

Leaders can facilitate a culture of trust in a number of ways, even within large organizations. First, there needs to be alignment around the company's shared objectives and purpose. Second, roles and responsibilities need to be clearly defined from the outset, leaving no room for buck passing or finger pointing down the line. Third, opportunities need to be designated to review a project's progress toward its stated goal, and benchmarks, acceleration points, and off-ramps must be established that remove bias and ego from decisions regarding when to invest more or when to cut losses and move on. Fourth, it's important that we begin placing as much value on being a strong follower and team member as we do on being a strong leader. Fifth, leaders should strive to identify and weed out bias throughout their organizations as much as possible and to foster a more equitable working environment for all. Finally, leaders need to champion transparency and accountability from top to bottom.

Those who get a taste of what it's like to work in a small but highly effective team—where camaraderie runs high and trust is the initial condition— often yearn for those days long after they're gone. Growth in most cases is a positive, but we can't ignore the adverse impact it can have on team dynamics. Taking these steps will go a long way in bringing a startup-like level of trust and alignment back into larger organizations.

Recommendation: If you're mentoring young professionals, hand them a copy of Patrick Lencioni's *The Five Dysfunctions of a Team*, and stress the importance of establishing trust in the business community. Use your own experiences as a guide, and tell them stories of how damaging mistrust can be for a team and for a business. You can make a difference in the trajectory of future leaders by helping to open their minds to the importance of organizational trust and the benefits of a proper technical/behavioral skill balance.

When Everyone's in Charge, No One's in Charge

You've all been there. It's Thursday afternoon, and you're part of a text message chain with a group of friends trying to figure out where to go to dinner. Each member has an opinion but is afraid to share it—the chain goes around and around with "I don't care" or a buck-passing "It's up to you."

The same thing happens in a business setting. As traditional "command and control" (C&C) management systems are replaced with flattened, matrixed, collaborative systems, decision making and driving successful outcomes become more challenging. This is exacerbated by the expectation that all team members should be heard and their opinions considered before reaching compromise and consensus to move forward. I've seen more than my fair share of projects stall or fail because decisions were delayed or never materialized.

So how do you avoid the negative effects of the "when everyone's in charge, no one's in charge" modern management system?

Unless you're a sole proprietor or lead a very small company, complex organizations must employ some degree of matrix-structured format to be successful. Organizational matrices can be aligned around vectors like channel (e.g., B2B or B2C), product, geography, life cycle, and/or regulatory environment. Over time, silos and tribes form along these vectors, and collaboration becomes more difficult as egos and formal reporting structures get in the way of project success. Being a collaborative leader is a necessary condition for effective leadership in complex organizations but is not by itself sufficient.

I posit that a necessary condition for effective teamwork and collaboration is to strike a balance between leadership and followership. I define *followership* as the ability to actively listen, give/receive constructive criticism, make meaningful contributions to a team, take direction, and be accountable for agreed-upon action items.[1]

The point I'm driving at here is that in a complex, matrixed organization, sometimes you're the leader and sometimes you're a follower. The leader/follower proportions change as responsibility increases along one's career progression. When you start out in your career, you're primarily following, and as you move up in the organization, leadership responsibilities increase.

The challenge I'm pointing out is that as leadership skills are fostered and improved, followership skills tend not to be nurtured at the same rate—and they need to be—even though they are employed at a lower proportion. In our zeal to instill leadership traits into employees in all levels of an organization, we neglect to reinforce the value of being an effective follower.

Personally, I find it incredibly difficult to shift gears from leader to follower—primarily because I don't get to practice my followership skills as much as I do my leadership skills. A strong secondary reason (some would argue it's the primary reason) is that my ego has been conditioned over many years in leadership roles to assume that stance as the initial condition. I'm so used to being the boss that I subconsciously resist being a follower. I

---

1. Robert Kelley's *The Power of Followership* (1992) was one of the first books published on the subject, but there are many other definitions and references out there.

have to pull my followership skills into conscious working memory and actively deploy them to be a better listener and team member.

Businesses are powered by people, and people make decisions—thousands of them every day. Successful businesses make, on average, more good decisions than bad. Gaining consensus among team members is important to create buy-in on a decision or strategy, but at some point, someone has to decide what to do and where to go. Often, energy is expended gathering data and opinions only to see the initiative fail to get off the ground because the group doesn't want to hurt Suzie's feelings or give Billy what they perceive to be bad news.

In fact, a 1944 field memo on institutional sabotage distributed by the CIA to help its covert operatives during World War II recommended "referring all matters to committees for further study and consideration" as an effective strategy for stifling progress within large organizations.[2] Pause for a moment to visit the CIA website listed in the footnote. You'll likely be suprised by the modern-day relevance of the recommendations made in 1944!

Defining in writing up front who is responsible, accountable, consulted, and informed (RACI) can be an effective tool to mitigate the risk of inaction in cross-functional team environments where collaboration, empowerment, and groupthink are important. For larger initiatives, developing a project charter can be a good way to identify roles and responsibilities, with designated decision-making authority a key component of the charter.

Creating these documents can slow down progress initially, but they are invaluable tools to fall back on when entropy starts setting in mid-project and team members lose sight of stated goals and objectives. The charter

---

2. "Timeless Tips for 'Simple Sabotage,'" July 12, 2012; cia.gov/news-information/featured-story-archive/2012-featured-story-archive/simple-sabotage.html

Part 5: Alignment

and RACI should be treated as living documents, not to be stuffed in a drawer or filed away in a shared folder never to be seen again. On a periodic basis, they should be reviewed for accuracy and relevance and adjusted as necessary. Keeping these documents fresh can serve to remind team members how decisions are made and who makes them. These documents also place front and center the key performance indicators (KPIs) that can be used to promote accountability and alignment.

Another important step toward organizational alignment is self-exploration. I suggest making time on your next vacation or during the quiet periods on a weekend for exploring your own ego. Is it preventing you from being an effective follower? Is an inflated view of self getting in the way of being a team player? Before you embark on this self-reflection, give Ryan Holiday's *Ego Is the Enemy* a quick read. It will help remind you that respect for others is a key to success.

It's also important to spend time practicing being a follower. Your voice can still be heard, you can make your opinions known, and you can still influence the outcome. However, when the decision is made by the individuals defined as "responsible and accountable" in the RACI, it's important to shift into follower mode and make the contributions to the project you committed to in the project charter.

As you can probably tell, I'm not a fan of groupthink and group decision making when it results in indecision and paralysis. I am a fan of gathering opinions, gaining consensus, and driving results.

Businesses need leaders and followers in the right proportions and at the right time. The best leaders and team contributors are the ones who have the emotional and intellectual intelligence to know when and how to apply effective leadership and followership. Following can be uncomfortable, but adopting and practicing this skill is essential in complex, matrixed organizations.

Nearly Stranded at LaGuardia

On a recent business trip, I asked several immediate family members to join me so they could enjoy the fruits of the Big Apple while I worked, and then we could spend our evenings together.

Specifically, I wanted them to attend the Kaplan Educational Foundation (KEF) Gala to see firsthand the great work the Foundation[3] does to help individuals from challenging backgrounds achieve life-changing educational goals for themselves and their families. It was a wonderful evening in which KEF scholars told their stories. We honored the achievements of two larger-than-life figures in the educational landscape—my friend and colleague John Polstein of Kaplan and Michael Sorrell of Paul Quinn College. It was a fabulous evening. Box checked!

As is the usual course when I travel with family, the night before we returned home, I planned our departure times for the next morning and informed everyone when we were to meet for breakfast as well as the time we had to be in the cab to make our way to LaGuardia Airport. That evening, our son Nick's girlfriend, Emily, showed me a notification she had received from Delta regarding the boarding time of our flight. It was an hour earlier than what I had planned, so I told her that she was likely still looking at the notification she had when we were still on Central Time.

The next morning, we awoke at the appointed time and began preparing for the trip home. Emily sent me a text with another notification that showed our departure time at 10:48 a.m. My wife's itinerary showed the same time, but my app was indicating our departure was an hour later, at 11:48 a.m.

I immediately felt awful that I had doubted and, frankly, completely dismissed Emily the night before. My attention now turned to potential problems with my app. I was determined to let Delta know how upset I

---

3. To learn more, visit http://www.kaplanedfoundation.org

was that their systems had been showing me incorrect departure times, causing us to almost miss our flight.

We wolfed down a few breakfast bars that Linda had in her bag and scrambled to the airport. Thankfully, my wife always has emergency calories in her bag.

When we arrived at the airport, I went through the TSA PreCheck line instead of slogging through regular security with the family so I could see what was going on with our flight. On the other side, I checked the monitor, and to my great dismay, I discovered there were *two* flights to the Minneapolis–St. Paul Airport that morning—one departing at 10:48 a.m. and the other at 11:48 a.m. Because I was traveling on business, I was on a separate record from the rest of the family, but I had assumed there were no errors in booking. It never dawned on me that I might have been booked on another flight. Sure enough, I had been inadvertently placed on the 11:48 a.m., and my family was on the flight exactly an hour earlier.

Now I was feeling even worse—I had dismissed Emily the night before, and that morning I was ready to give Delta a piece of my mind about their error. All along, the problem was with *me*.

Britannica defines *confirmation bias* as "the tendency to process information by looking for, or interpreting, information that is consistent with one's existing beliefs."[4] In this case, I'm pretty confident that I was looking at the situation through the lens of "Andy the world traveler." How could Emily possibly know more than I did about our itinerary? I was the one who had booked their travel and was certain that I'd relayed the right flight numbers to my executive assistant to book mine.

Worse yet, as I delve deeper into the erroneous thinking that led me to almost steer the whole family astray that day, I see that I may have also

---

4. *Confirmation Bias*, Bettina J. Casad, 2007; britannica.com/science/confirmation-bias

been biased by age. I'm older and more experienced. Emily is young and can't possibly know better. Right? Wrong.

Confirmation bias is insidious because it lives primarily in one's subconscious mind. I like to *think* I have an open mind and take onboard information from multiple sources before making decisions. I try to be fair and balanced, actively listen, and keep my ego in check. However, I'm sure my subconscious is littered with belief structures that impede my ability to make the best decisions possible. For example, I'm sure I've opted out of wonderful experiences because my subconscious was telling me, "You wouldn't like that. Remember back in 1994 when so-and-so did such-and-such and you hated it?"

The horrifying thing about this particular experience with Emily is that I've started to look back and think about how many conclusions I've jumped to over the years based on long-standing beliefs. I'm certain I owe Linda a thousand apologies for my confirmation bias. Fortunately, most of us suffer from confirmation bias, so she probably only owes me five hundred (yes, she's that much better than I am).

Now, let's mix ego, hierarchy, departments, divisions, and all the trappings of the corporate world into our story. Each of the humans that populates your business comes to the table with a different background, educational track record, and talents. Your teammates also come pre-wired with a unique set of confirmation biases based on their environment, upbringing, and experiences. Ideally, they bring their whole self to work and see the world through their own unique lens.

To get a sense of the variability of the thought processes and points of view found within your organization, start with your team. Let's say you're the team lead, and you have five direct reports. Let's assume each team member (including you) has three distinct confirmation biases that color decision making on how a particular problem is approached. The probability that each team member will interpret a particular scenario in the same way is low.[5] You might think the team gels and is on the same page, but statistically, the level of variability—even among what might appear to be a small, homogeneous team—is high.

Now imagine a business with a hundred, a thousand, or ten thousand employees. The likelihood that the whole organization views a challenge in the same way is functionally zero. If we ignore for a moment that each individual navigates through change at a different pace, confirmation bias is all the proof you should need to see why change management in an organizational setting is so incredibly difficult. Even if *nothing* changes, the current state of the business will be viewed in myriad ways, with multiple solutions offered to solve current challenges. Add in substantive change, and you've got a real jumble of attitudes, perspectives, and viewpoints.

Hopefully, you're having an "ah-ha" moment regarding change management, communication, alignment, and active listening. As you may recall from part 3, the old marketing "rule of seven" has been applied in corporate communications. I've used it too—surely team members will hear and properly interpret a message after I've repeated it seven times. Again, wrong. Due to all the variability of thought, opinion, and bias that lives within an organization, it likely will take seventy times to get a message through.[6]

I've personally been in a room with team members where I would deliver what I thought was a crisp, clean, unassailable message. The team would greet the message with enthusiasm and what appeared to be universal agreement. Days or weeks later, I'd have team members come back to me with very different interpretations of what I had meant to get across. In some cases, this would happen over and over again. There have been

---

5. You presumably know your confirmation bias, but there's a one in three chance for a particular bias in each of the other five members of the team. You're effectively rolling a three-sided die. Hence, the probability that everyone applies the same bias to a particular problem is $0.33^5 = 0.004$ or 0.4%.

6. I'm being dramatic here. It might not be seventy, but it is certainly more than seven.

times in my career where this obstinance was intentional, but in the vast majority of cases, the disconnect was completely unintended. Instead, the message was likely running into a confirmation bias the recipient had (that we were both unaware of), which made interpretation and acceptance of the message difficult.

As a leader, I've found that effective communication is the most difficult part of my role. Yes, it's never easy to give challenging feedback or terminate an employee, but those are episodic components of my role at best. However, I find the necessity to repeat myself in different ways through different modalities very difficult. How many of you have whispered under your breath, "I've already said 'x' twice! Why don't they get it?" I recommend you learn from my mistakes. Search for the joy in finding creative ways of repeating yourself to ensure your messages are received and understood.

One way to help solve confirmation bias in an organization is to ensure everyone is speaking the same language—not English or French, but the language of your business. This is where continuous improvement and the four core competencies discussed in part 2 come into play.

Injecting the tenets of continuous improvement (CI) into your organization will help ensure all team members are using a common set of tools to frame and solve problems, taking some of the guesswork out of interpreting what is being said. A CI journey is not a panacea or a silver bullet, but adopting a common language has certainly helped the organizations I've led.

As discussed in part 3, we all wear a one-size-fits-you pair of lenses that colors how we send and receive information. In addition to the four recommendations given previously to minimize the Lensing Effect, I'd like to add fighting confirmation bias to the list. After all, without solving for confirmation bias, alignment is nearly impossible to achieve, especially in large organizations.

To minimize confirmation bias, I recommend that you start with you. Spend some time in deep reflection exploring your beliefs and past experiences. Ask yourself how those experiences and beliefs may create unintended bias in how you view the world or approach problem solving. Only after you've explored your own belief system and how it creates challenges in interpreting data can you start thinking about how the beliefs of others color their lenses. Not to get too philosophical, but the world will be a better and less polarized place if we all work to understand our sources of potential confirmation bias.

The topic of confirmation bias is a devilishly tricky subject to tackle in a corporate environment because confirmation bias is influenced by beliefs and experiences that intersect with race, culture, sexual orientation, and age, just to name a few. As a leader, all I can do is explore *my* potential sources of bias and recognize that those around me wear their own unique lenses through which they view the world. I can make educated guesses at potential confirmation biases in other people based on what I know about them, but that's all they are—educated guesses.[7]

We had a great time in New York. The Kaplan team did great work, and my family got to hear inspirational Kaplan Educational Foundation stories as well as see two awesome Broadway productions.

I've since apologized profusely to Emily, and the experience was a real wake-up call for me to be a better human by working on my own trigger points for confirmation bias.

Now, where did I leave my rose-colored glasses?

---

7. And I need to be careful, because these educated guesses can turn into more confirmation bias!

Lost in a Sea of Ragweed

When I was ten years old, my parents put me on the Amtrak from La Crosse to Minneapolis to visit my cousin Joe. The time of year was late August—the perfect point in the summer to give my folks a rest from their precocious son before the school year started.

Some of my fondest memories are of Joe and me camping out in the backyard of my aunt and uncle's house in Brooklyn Park. It was a big, foreign land filled with unfamiliar noises that kept us up all night. We would listen to the radio, streak[8] through the neighbor's yard, and pretend that we were in the middle of nowhere, left to fend for ourselves.

Joe and I were also terrible allergy sufferers. By morning, our tent would be filled with used facial tissues, and neither of us could breathe. We would retreat back into the air-conditioning to recuperate until sundown, and the lunacy would start all over.

After the third night, we went back into the house, and my aunt let out a shriek! My head had swollen up like a basketball. After too much of a good thing, my body was revolting against all the pollen. As you might imagine, my parents jumped into the car to retrieve me. The next day, I found myself at the allergy specialist getting poked and prodded with little needles filled with various allergens. The culprits were ragweed and goldenrod—my nemeses to this day.

Fast forward to late August of 2019: Linda and I live on a bluff top just outside La Crosse, Wisconsin. It's an idyllic setting, with a small, groomed yard surrounding the house, encircled by roughly four acres of wildflowers. Patches of my enemies crop up in various places amid the wildflowers, and I have a very short window in mid-August to cut them down before they go to seed.

---

8. Yes, you read that right. Ray Stevens's song "The Streak" was a big hit at the time.

Each summer, I dress in jeans and a long-sleeved shirt, put on my hat and gloves, and top off the look with an industrial-strength breathing mask to capture as much of the insidious pollen as possible. My tool of choice is a Stihl® trimmer with a metal blade on the end for maximum devastation.

Before I start cutting, I map my route through the field and solicit Linda's opinion on where I'll find the most offending plants to ensure the most efficient and effective results. With this mental map and my armor, I'm ready for battle!

That year, after about two hours in the field, I found myself randomly attacking individual plants with my blade—I had lost track of the big clumps of weeds and was just flailing away. I paused, turned off the trimmer, removed my mask, and sighed.

I realized I had lost track of my route and was wasting energy and time grinding individual plants into a pulp. The work was helping me *feel* like I was making progress—I was indeed very busy and very sweaty—but I wasn't making an impact.

You might be asking yourself, "Andy, why does this story matter to my role as a leader or manager?"

I stood there in the weeds, struck by how many times in my career I had lost perspective. I would be grinding away at my work, feeling productive, but the work I was engaged in really didn't matter or wasn't aligned with the end goal. Note that I'm not talking about getting distracted—to me, that's a completely different subject. Distraction is a temporary dalliance from the work at hand and is more easily rectified. Being lost is something completely different.

Before you continue reading, I invite you to reflect on a time in business when you or your team lost sight of a goal.

Many humans I know like to check boxes. They like order and routine. They like seeing things through and proceeding one step at a time. They like seeing results and making progress. It runs against many of our personality types to step back and ask whether the work we're doing is still adding the value it was intended to. It's really hard for most humans to admit failure or stop a project midstream. We're all taught the concept of sunk costs in Economics 101. However, it's much more challenging to label work as a sunk cost, stop that work, move on to more productive endeavors, *and* be ok with it.

When I was in the field, it struck me how many times I have seen this behavior in the past—and how it was still occurring in the present, despite the company's best efforts to engage in continuous improvement practices to root out and eliminate waste. It's this human desire to bring closure to projects that can generate waste in organizations. We either subconsciously reject the economic principle of sunk cost or justify to ourselves that "we're this far, we might as well drive the project to conclusion" when we know full well that we're just wasting time and resources doing so.

To avoid or reduce the likelihood that your team will get lost analyzing individual pieces of bark on the trees in the forest, I recommend you consider the following:

1. Develop "off-ramps" before you start a group project, and gather consensus on the best opportunities to stop for review and consideration. When we start projects or establish goals, we seldom clearly define the trigger points that will lead us to reassess trajectory or redeploy resources to higher and better uses. We get emotionally attached to our work, and emotion tends to cloud our thinking. If you define the metrics and trigger points that determine whether the project moves forward on a prespecified future date, emotional bias will be reduced, and clearer heads

will prevail. If the project is big enough, consider employing a review board to provide an outside perspective.

2. Gather your team at the departmental or project gemba board on a biweekly basis (or a cadence that makes sense for the scope and scale of the work).[9] Encourage open and honest feedback from team members regarding what's going well and what's not. If you routinely sweep challenging feedback under the rug, you'll end up ignoring sunk costs and your team members will stop providing critical feedback, because they won't believe it will be acted upon.

3. Empower your project managers. Most project managers view their role as one of keeping the trains running on time, ensuring smooth handoffs between teams, and reducing unnecessary duplication of effort. We must also empower our project managers to ask critical questions regarding a project's health and whether the project is likely to yield its intended return on investment.

4. Carve out time for contemplation and reflection. If you find yourself always powering through or are so busy that you can't think critically, this is your first sign that you're at risk of losing sight of what really matters. This applies to both business and personal life. My favorite place to do this is on bicycle rides through the coulees of La Crosse County.

To get started, you may find it helpful to ask the following questions regarding the projects you're working on and the goals you've set for yourself and your team:

---

9. As mentioned in part 2, gemba boards offer a visual representation of an individual's or team's progress toward predetermined benchmarks and goals. Visit the Lean Enterprise Institute (https://www.lean.org/) for more information on gemba boards.

1. Is the work still relevant? When did we last ask this question in a team meeting? When is the last time we conferred with management or leaders of other functional areas on the value of our work?

2. Are we emotionally attached to the work? Is that emotion clouding our thinking? Do we harbor unconscious bias that needs to be addressed?

3. Have we empowered all team members with a voice? Do we listen to those voices or simply pay them lip service?

4. Do we feel like we're caught on a treadmill? Spinning but going nowhere? Step off and reflect. Where's your favorite place for contemplation and reflection?

When I was in the field with my big trimmer, I should have taken several short breaks to reassess my progress and the impact I was making (or lack thereof). I should have been willing to stop my work earlier and develop a different plan if I was being ineffective.

I must have looked ridiculous, standing in the field dressed like a lumberjack, staring aimlessly off into the distance. After what seemed like a long time, I walked out of the field, reconvened with Linda on where I went wrong, and then proceeded to dispatch clumps of ragweed with efficiency and efficacy.

And before you start writing me letters, I understand that during fall allergy season, pollen is floating in the air from ragweed plants from miles around and my efforts to knock them down around the house are likely futile. I gain significant benefit (albeit irrational) from the activity because it helps me feel like I'm making a difference. Control what I can . . .

Linda, where's the Flonase®?

The True North of Indispensability

In late 2018, Linda and I went out to Portland, Oregon, for a few days to visit our son Brandon. During our time together, we visited several Willamette Valley wineries with an expectation that we would join a wine club.[10]

We visited three wineries during our tour, and initial impressions at each location were favorable. As you might imagine, the wineries were all nestled into gorgeous surroundings. Their facilities were well kept and inviting, but the similarities stopped there.

At Wineries A and C, the staff were courteous and extremely knowledgeable about their products. They took time to help us feel welcome and included—like we were the only clients they had seen all day and genuinely wanted us to have a great experience. They were confident, but not overly so. They also knew the science behind what they were selling and were able to explain it in layperson's terms. Most important, their products backed up their claims.

At Winery B, the staff clearly wished they were somewhere else. They didn't seem to know the local area and certainly weren't trained in wine tasting or the science of wine. Their sales pitch was nothing special, and when pressed for more information, their lack of depth became acutely obvious to us. Worse yet, the product didn't stand up to the hype. The Willamette Valley is known for its Pinot Noir, but their product was thin and lacked substance. Both the people and the product failed to live up to expectations.

Remember, we started the day as prospective buyers, expecting to join a wine club. We ended up joining clubs at both Wineries A and C because they created a positive environment, made us feel included, and delivered

---

10. A wine club is a "cancel anytime" agreement for the buyer to receive two to four shipments of wine per year from the seller. In return for membership in the club, the buyer receives discounted prices and access to members-only communication and events.

a wonderful product. Do we need to belong to two wine clubs? Probably not. Will we end up as a long-term member of each club? That depends on how reliably each company delivers an extraordinary experience in the future. If their follow-through isn't there or consistency wanes, it will be easy for us to switch. However, as time goes by, our relationships with Wineries A and C are likely to strengthen—creating stickiness between buyer and seller.

These types of relationships are common. Gas is a commodity—easily exchanged for alternative vendors—but the entire convenience store experience is not. You go to the same convenience store over and over because of the consistency and reliability of its people and its products. You *become* a fan of brands because of great advertising, word-of-mouth recommendations, or an initial experience like the ones I outlined above. You *remain* a fan of brands when the proof points pile up. Switching becomes harder as the emotional bond strengthens.

A brand hits the jackpot when a sense of *indispensability* is created in the eyes of the consumer.

I'm sure you can all think of brands that you would have a difficult time switching away from because of the tight emotional and economic bonds that have been fostered over years of transactions.

I am convinced that one of the best weapons against transactional commoditization is to align around creating indispensable experiences for your business's consumers.[11] In my opinion, there are three key elements of indispensability: people, product, and reliability. When companies are small, shared goals and values are easy to establish. As companies expand,

---

11. A product or service that has become commoditized is indistinguishable from those offered by competitors. For commodities, lowering price is the primary method to achieve differentiation, so only companies with a low cost base survive in the long term. To justify higher prices and greater profitability, we must create real or perceived product differentiation to avoid getting caught in price wars with our competition. Continuous transformation is key.

aligning around a singular vision of indispensability becomes more difficult but all the more important.

The following discussion centers around indispensability in the education industry. However, it shouldn't be difficult for you to think of examples relevant to your sector.

People

Here's the thread that ties education to wine—they're both examples of service industries.[12] People are the ingredient that defines excellence in any service economy. That's why Kaplan's team members are its most valuable asset. We can have the coolest technology and the fanciest book covers, but none of that matters if we're not consistently passionate and knowledgeable about what we do. This applies to everyone who works for Kaplan, irrespective of job category or rank.

If you ask the custodial technician at Walt Disney World what her job is, she's likely to answer, "To create memorable experiences for our guests," as she empties the trash inside Space Mountain. That's because *everyone* plays a part in creating memorable experiences at Disney. Providing a consistent experience across the brand is valued and nurtured as a key part of the customer's experience.

To reinforce this point to our team members, I routinely repeat a version of the following statement, "When you wake up each day and 'punch in' to work, remind yourself that you're going to help create life-changing moments for hundreds, if not thousands, of students today. You're going to help a corporate administrator solve an educational challenge and/or help a family build a stronger economic foundation through education and learning. Today, and every day, you're going to make a difference."

---

12. Technically, education is a hybrid industry that spans both service and product.

There are many articles about purpose and meaning in the workplace. There's literally a book entitled *Purpose and Meaning in the Workplace*.[13] At Kaplan, we don't have to manufacture purpose in our work; it's built right in. Everyone, from Laura to Andy, plays an integral part.

Product

Education is a strange animal because we're both a service and a product industry. We create intellectual property and package content into educational experiences. If our people represent our most valuable asset, then our intellectual property is second. We can have the most welcoming and inclusive buying experiences, but if we're not creating the outcomes that matter to our students and clients, what's the point?

Ten years ago, during the "massive open online course" (MOOC) movement,[14] there were all sorts of predictions that content would be free and ubiquitous. Many believed training markets would die because individuals would curate their own experiences from the wealth of free material that would flood the market. While we've seen a plethora of new educational delivery models pop up over the last decade and plenty of free material, I'm happy to report that quality content, delivered by a reputable brand, still matters.

Where we will win is in our ability to measure outcomes and efficacy through our data and analytics capabilities. If we show the market consistently better results through the application of learning engineering and the Kaplan Way, we win.

---

13. Written by Bryan J. Dik, edited by Zinta S. Byrne and Michael F. Steger, published by the American Psychological Association on May 15, 2013.

14. Virtual educational content and experiences offered for free and open to anyone over the internet, often accompanied by forums and discussion boards where students and educators could collaborate and discuss problems or receive feedback and assistance from anywhere around the world.

While this discussion has centered around Kaplan's product offerings, I can't think of a market where product quality doesn't matter over the long term.

Reliability

Folks shake their heads when they hear that I would frequent the same restaurant for lunch most days of the week. What I liked about the experience is that I felt at home (people), the food was of high quality (product), and there were no surprises (reliability). There are so many variables in my life that trusting this restaurant with my lunch choices took one more detail off my plate. I value reliability. I also get teased about my wardrobe, but my Garanimals-style of dressing works for me. Banana Republic non-iron dress shirts, work-appropriate Express[15] jeans or JoS. A. Bank slacks, and a matching sport coat is the formula that takes the guesswork out of getting dressed in the morning!

Again, think about the brands you love—especially the ones you rely on day in, day out. I would guess that a key driver of your loyalty to those brands is that they don't let you down. This is especially critical in education—students and clients are placing a great deal of trust in us when they choose Kaplan. Consistency is key.

In continuous improvement parlance, a company's "true north" is the vision or purpose of the organization. It's the mission that aligns each of its unique team members. Kaplan's is to "help individuals achieve their educational and career goals. We build futures, one success story at a time."

Indispensability is the key to our true north, and it's the key to clients and learners coming back to us again and again throughout their lifelong

15. I'm currently struggling with ALL brands of men's jeans. Apparently, the source manufacturer of jean material decided that all consumers would like the new stretchy material they're currently producing. Your only choice today is "stretchy" or "more stretchy." I don't like the stretch, and I'm a very dissatisfied customer. Tell me how you really feel, Andy . . .

learning journeys. Indispensability means that a learner or client says, "I need my Kaplan." It means that we are so good along the entire value chain that there are no effective substitutes for our products and services. It means that we stand alone in the consideration set.

By defining and living the values that make us indispensable to our clients and customers, we can easily align around our true north, no matter how much the company grows in the future.

Think about your own industry and your own business. What does indispensability mean to you?

PART 6

Leader Standard Work

It was a beautiful sunny day in Iowa City, Iowa. The date—July 1989. The golden dome on the Old Capitol shone like a beacon in the bright sun. My wife, Linda, took up temporary residence with a good book under one of the large pine trees that were scattered across the Pentacrest. My task that day was to interview with the chair of the finance department at the University of Iowa, one of ten graduate schools of finance I had applied to after graduating from the University of Wisconsin–La Crosse (UW–L) with a degree in economics. It was my only interview.

I was acutely feeling the pressure that resulted from my decision to apply to graduate school immediately after earning my undergraduate degree. I had received letters of rejection from Michigan, Northwestern, Wisconsin, and Minnesota—primarily due to my lack of work experience and a great, but not outstanding, GMAT score. Having been near the top of my class as an undergraduate, the experience was a lesson in humility and a reality check regarding the level of competition I was up against.

I kissed Linda goodbye and made my way to Phillips Hall—then the home of the business school—and headed up to the top floor. Bev, the department secretary, greeted me with a smile and escorted me into the finance chair's office, where I was met by a tall, lanky gentleman in his mid-forties. He shook my hand and asked me to sit opposite him at his side table by the window. I looked out, and there was Linda under the tree amid the beautiful scene that surrounded her. At that moment, all the pressure melted away. I felt like I was home.

You see, at UW–L, I was bitten hard by the teaching bug. After my first year there, I knew that teaching at the collegiate level would be a good fit for me and that grad school was in my future. My father was a teacher and an administrator at the local technical school, and my mother was a corporate trainer, so I had a good idea of what I'd be getting into. I suspected my early experiences as a singer and performer were likely to translate into the classroom as well.

What was supposed to be a one-hour interview turned into two, but the time passed effortlessly. The chair and I had a broad-ranging discussion about my aspirations to be a finance professor, and he coached me on why I didn't get interviews from the other schools. He pressed me on my motivations but was simultaneously open and approachable. He didn't lecture me, but made it clear I had hard work ahead of me if I was going to succeed. He emphasized that I'd be at a disadvantage to the other students, but also gave me hope and was clear about what I had to do to close the gap. Apparently, the finance chair saw the light in my eyes and the potential I had because by the end of the conversation, he had granted me conditional entry into the program.

Over the course of the next six years, the bond between me and the finance chair would grow. He was tough but fair, and, in retrospect, it seemed like he always made time for me when I needed it. As I look back, there was a unique balance to the relationship—he was fact based and objective but also seemed to care deeply about my success. I know I wasn't his only student, but there were times when it felt like I was. He was truly gifted at developing talent. His name is Carl Schweser.

As you've probably gathered, Carl and I would go on to found the Schweser Study Program for the CFA Exams, and both our wives would play critical roles in the development of the business. What started with an interview for graduate school in 1989 turned into a lasting friendship and a business that was sold to Kaplan a decade later. I am who I am today because of Carl and a handful of other extraordinary human beings who saw something in me that I couldn't see in myself at a particular stage of my life.[1] They all played their parts in their own ways and at different times, helping me develop an understanding of effective, ethical, and balanced leadership. I am eternally grateful to all of them.

The Value of a Professional Continuous Improvement Journey

In the category of "I wish I knew then what I know now," having even a rudimentary set of continuous improvement tools to rely on during the more challenging early periods of my life would have been extremely helpful. The road would have been a little less bumpy and certainly less stressful.

The tools of continuous improvement, when applied to a business environment, can be extremely effective in keeping teams focused on identifying and rooting out waste, respecting team members, and keeping the customer at the fore. As we wove continuous improvement philosophies deeper into the business operations at Kaplan, I found that those same concepts applied in spades to my personal life. Just as the tenets of marriage counseling are highly effective when applied to nurturing healthy

---

1. Dan Johnson-Wilmot, Mike Marsh, Keith Sherony, Roger Leithold, and my mother and father. I list my mom and dad on purpose—many parents shirk their responsibility to mentor their children. While parenting is a much broader role, a key component of the parent-child relationship is mentoring.

teams, the concepts of continuous improvement are applicable to life outside of the office.

Once you adopt a continuous improvement mindset, waste becomes visible everywhere, as do opportunities to improve even the most basic tasks and processes. You begin to examine every aspect of your long-established routines. For example, you consider why you take three trips back and forth from the fridge as you make your breakfast in the morning when, with some careful planning, you could just take one. The minuscule time savings might hardly seem worth the effort, but when you consider the impact of that slight efficiency improvement over the course of multiple days, weeks, months, or years—and then combine it with other small and seemingly insignificant improvements—the cumulative effect can be significant. For example, let's say you also discover a way to reorganize your closet to make getting ready in the morning more efficient. Perhaps after taking the same route to work for years, you decide to second-guess that habit, and guess what? It turns out there's a slightly more direct commute. You might be thinking to yourself, "So what? All of this effort to save what, fifteen minutes in the morning, what's the big deal?"

That's a fair question, but consider what you could do with an extra fifteen minutes each day and the effect it could have on the rest of your day. Maybe you're able to get a little bit of exercise, spend some time catching up on the news before work, spend more time around the breakfast table with your family, or even just get a few extra minutes of sleep. When added up, these extra few minutes can be put toward activities that can have a dramatic impact on your overall health and well-being in both the short and long terms.[2] Just consider the cumulative effect of getting just fifteen minutes of exercise in the morning for one, five, ten, or fifteen years. It could literally extend your lifespan, all because you got into the habit of

---

2. One of the most successful Victorian novelists, Anthony Trollope, wrote forty-seven novels in fifteen-minute increments! (Source: *250 Words Every 15 Minutes*, James R. Kincaid, December 22, 1991: *New York Times*.)

taking the milk, eggs, and cheese out from the fridge together, rather than one by one (plus plenty of other time-saving habits, of course).

The same is true in business operations: the results of continuous improvement range from the nearly imperceptible to dramatic sea changes. The beauty of continuous improvement is the reliable set of tools that leaders and individual contributors amass over time and the common language that gets adopted across the organization. This codification of processes and problem solving improves organizational trust and bolsters accountability. In an organization that's adopted continuous improvement and organizational health principles, it becomes increasingly difficult to hide mediocrity and substandard performance.

When continuous improvement tools are applied on a personal level, mistakes are recognized and corrected more rapidly. Over time, your eyes become accustomed to seeing fault points and recognizing the impact of your actions on others. It's tough to be self-absorbed and blind to the fallout of your actions if you're managing for daily improvement (MDI), aware of your current state, and executing a plan to achieve a desired future state. On a personal level, this amounts to physically looking at yourself in the mirror and asking two simple questions, "How will I be a better person today than I was yesterday?" and "Am I making progress toward my goals?"

Before you can answer these questions, it's important to take a look back at yesterday and honestly assess situations that didn't go quite the way they should have. This willingness and ability to critically reflect (not dwell) on the past is a routine we should all adopt. Put the cell phone down, close Facebook, and meditate on your prior actions. Try to place yourself in the shoes of those you've interacted with, and think about how they may have interpreted your actions and words. Your ability to self-assess the previous day will improve over time if you're constantly building your situational awareness and emotional intelligence muscles.

The sooner you learn that behavioral skills are of equal (or greater) importance to the technical skills you learned in school, the better off you'll be as a team member, leader, friend, spouse, and parent.

If you're a mentor and a guide to those around you, I recommend you introduce the concepts behind continuous improvement to your mentees. Discuss with them how consistent, incremental improvements can pay big dividends down the road—that the understanding of self and one's relationship with others can have a tremendous return on investment—in business and in life outside the office. Ask mentees to physically look in the mirror and ask the two questions posed above. Then help them make sense of their responses. This is likely to be difficult but highly rewarding work as you help build great future citizens.

Ethical Leadership

My former role as CEO of Kaplan Professional, when stripped down to its most bare components, was to maximize current-period revenue and operating profit for Kaplan. But, to quote Don Graham, chairman of the Graham Holdings Company, "Companies grow with the money they make." This means that the work we do to maximize current-period operating profit is balanced against a long-term vision for the company.

If you remove external factors like government subsidies, regulations, and other "unnatural" parts of the economic equation, no business is able to survive without the ability to generate profits; profits that can be plowed back into the business to develop new products and services, explore new markets, and foster growth.

Viewed through the lens of ethical leadership, the task of generating profits should be balanced with the needs of customers and employees. Without customers and employees, the business will ultimately fail. The inclusive, frank, and fearless environment that we're striving to build therefore needs to be balanced against the profit motive, accountability, and responsiveness.

Historically speaking, leaders have held a lot of unchecked power over their staff. There has generally been a disconnect between the opportunity, joy, and purpose of their teams and the company's ability to succeed as a business in purely economic terms. More recently, however, that balance of power has been completely flipped on its head, and we're now dealing with the effects of an overcorrection.

Thanks to multibillion-dollar "unicorn"[3] employers in Silicon Valley and elsewhere—as well as the "everyone gets a prize" culture that they grew up in—many young(er) people believe that they deserve to work for an organization that caters to their every need. A study by the Society for Human Resource Management (SHRM) found that roughly a third of Gen Z[4] employees demand a say over their work schedules, more than one-third "won't tolerate" being forced to work when they don't want to— or being denied the vacation days they request—and slightly less than a third would refuse to work back-to-back shifts. At the same time, nearly a third of the 3,000 Gen Z survey respondents surveyed across eleven countries believes they are members of the hardest-working generation in the workforce.[5]

In recent years, I've seen more and more candidates walk through the door with an attitude that suggests the employer should feel lucky that this rock star employee is willing to grace them with their presence and that if the business can't wow them, they'll take their talents somewhere that has an in-house caterer, free exercise classes, and a mini-golf course.[6] The employment standards set by the unicorns have built employment

---

3. A "unicorn" company is defined as a privately held startup valued at over $1 billion.
4. The generation following Millennials, born between the mid-to-late 1990s and the early 2010s.
5. *Generation Z Says They Work the Hardest, But Only When They Want To,* by Dana Wilkie on June 11, 2019, at SHRM.org
6. Google's Toronto-based Canadian headquarters actually has a mini-golf course on its roof!

expectations that are unachievable and unsustainable for most employers—much like Ken and Barbie did for physical body standards in the 1960s and beyond.

The problem with the "everybody's a winner" mentality is that some of the world's greatest success stories come from those who have failed time and time again, and only struck gold when they were able to understand and learn from those failures. Bill Gates's first company failed, Steve Jobs was let go from Apple, and Walt Disney was fired from his job at a newspaper because his boss felt he lacked creativity. Author Stephen King used to hang rejection slips on a nail above his desk.[7] By the time he was fourteen, the nail could no longer support the weight of all those rejections, so he replaced it with a railroad spike and continued writing.

Silicon Valley leaders like to talk about embracing failure, but the reality is that with so much competition among employers, graduates have been led to believe that if their employer is unwilling to offer them their dream work experience, they should just bring their talents to the competitor next door.

To me, the poster child of this culture is the concept of unlimited paid time off (UPTO), which has become standard in many workplaces, especially among unicorn companies. As an aside, I think the whole concept of unlimited PTO is a complete farce. It creates an unwritten agreement that says, "Sure, take all the time off you want, but if you ask for too much, I'll begin to question your loyalty and commitment to your job."[8]

The point is that the balance between leadership and individual contributors is way out of whack. While historically too much power was in the

---

7. As described in his 2010 memoir, *On Writing.*
8. In fact, those with UPTO take, on average, two days less vacation than those with traditional vacation policies, according to a study conducted by Business Insider. The survey also found that 29% of employees with UPTO admit to "always" working on vacation, compared with only 15% of those with more traditional PTO arrangements. (Source: *Is unlimited vacation a trap? It just might be.* Angela Wang, June 21, 2019: Business Insider.)

hands of leadership, employees now feel they hold a certain power over their employers. Both attitudes are inherently flawed; I believe there must be a balanced give-and-take.

That's where continuous improvement comes in. Whether you're a leader or an individual contributor, the first step toward continuous improvement is understanding that you are accountable for your own development and improvement over time. Others will provide resources, mentorship, and guidance. However, without opening up to the idea that there is room for improvement—and that the journey toward improvement has value to you as an individual and a team member—it's impossible to make any progress.

Leaders aren't off the hook here, either. Too often they convince themselves that their role is more nebulous, less concretely defined, and ever changing, making them exempt from the task of continuous improvement. I'll be the first to admit that I've held this attitude in the past myself.

Our human nature thrives on comfort and reliability; we want to set a process and do it over and over again. We don't want to come into work tomorrow only to discover that our tried-and-true process is no longer good enough and needs to be reinvented. However, the longer a process is replicated without improvement, the more ingrained those habits become and the more difficult they are to break. That is why the clay layer, introduced in part 2, is so resistant to change: "Why should we be forced to fix something that's worked for so long and doesn't appear to be broken?"

The purpose of standard work is to document, in writing, your best current thinking about how a job should be done and then continuously iterate and improve on that process. In order for that to happen, employees need to shake off the impression that they're irreplaceable, special, and impervious to failure and accountability. At the same time, managers and leaders need to shake off the impression that continuous improvement journeys exist solely for the benefit of lower-ranking colleagues and that they—those managers and leaders—should be off the hook. That is the only way to foster a balanced working environment.

To me, ethical leadership is all about finding new ways of working, new ways of understanding and satisfying customer needs, and new ways of being a servant to the people who work with you. That is why establishing a set of standard work for leaders is an important step in building healthy, balanced, and resilient businesses.

Defining Your Leader Standard Work

Imagine your company produces one thing—Product X—for sale into the consumer market. There is a value stream associated with Product X that represents the activities and processes necessary to bring Product X to market. At each point along the value stream, value is added to the product or service. To visualize this, start with an idea, add raw materials, and refine those materials into the final product that is consumed in the market.

Value-stream mapping is the activity of identifying and documenting the high-level process steps under the current state to create Product X. When you map a value stream, you're looking to eliminate as many non-value-adding activities (waste) as possible while simultaneously optimizing value-adding activities to improve efficiency and quality. An outcome of a value-stream mapping event is a picture of the desired future state for the value stream, where a heightened level of efficiency or value is created by establishing better flow through the stream. In this desired future state, new standard work is defined, which replaces the previous best practice. To me, this represents the heart of continuous improvement.

Managers and leaders play an essential role in any value stream. Just like the definition of standard work for an individual or a team applies to a specific process or activity along the value stream, leaders must adopt their own standard work to ensure they are providing accurate, reliable, and repeatable guidance to their teams. You can have the most well-defined set of processes and the most awesome value-stream map, but if leaders function in an ad hoc or random manner, optimal flow along the stream cannot be achieved. In other words, a leader who injects chaos into a system is likely doing more harm than good.

As an INTP on the Myers-Briggs scale and a C/D on the DiSC Profile, I have historically been one of those managers who injects chaos into the system. C/Ds are notorious for overanalyzing a situation and taking too long to reach a decision. The introvert (I) in me also doesn't help, because I have not been constructively "frank and fearless" when I needed to be. I've come to realize that the more dependable and consistent I am in how I approach problem solving and decision making, the better off my teams are.

Note that adopting standard work doesn't mean you can't change your mind or respond to fluid market dynamics. It simply means you'll have a reliable framework within which shifting goals and business priorities are set and disseminated. Hence, I have direct evidence, accumulated over time, that performance improves when leaders adopt, and make public, their standard work.

Roughly a year after we embarked on our continuous improvement journey, my team and I held an offsite meeting to define the specific elements of our standard work. Unlike a process map or set of instructions, our leader standard work was a blend of high-level guiding principles and specific tasks, as follows.

Leaders at Kaplan Professional will do the following:

1. Teach, Coach, Mentor, and Inspire (TCMI)
2. Set and execute strategy (level appropriate)
3. Create and communicate clarity
4. Establish and monitor relevant key performance indicators
5. Fight entropy
6. Remove obstacles and help teams focus
7. Act as brand ambassadors

It's important to stress that the proportions of the leader standard work items listed above will vary substantially across the members of a team, and that those proportions are organization and level dependent. For example, my target proportions for each item listed above are skewed heavily toward the first three in the list. Our CFO would focus more on #4, and our head of sales would emphasize #6 and #7.

In addition, for leader standard work to be effective in practice, there should be a periodic feedback loop[9] in place where a leader looks at what he or she aspired to do, compares that to what actually happened, and adjusts as necessary. For example, you could aspire to spend 20 percent of your time as a brand ambassador but, in retrospect, realize that you only spent 5 percent of your time on those activities. As a continuous improvement leader, you would ask yourself why you did not achieve your goal and adjust your time allocations accordingly.

Much like the "Words I Live By" listing from part 4, the elements of your leader standard work may look very different from the list shown above. Through careful consideration, our leadership team defined a set of leader standard work that fit the culture, purpose, and objectives of Kaplan Professional, but each organization is unique. I hope our list inspires yours,

---

9. This feedback loop could take the form of a Plan, Do, Check, Act (PDCA) cycle.

but I strongly recommend you engage in a similar process for defining the leader standard work that best suits your organizational objectives.

I do, however, believe there are several immutable characteristics that should be part of *any* leader standard work. Focus must be placed on creating indispensable customer experiences, respecting and developing people, driving long-term business performance, and continuously improving business operations.

Furthermore, while the term *standard work* gives the connotation that it's fixed and unchangeable, nothing could be further from the truth. Your leader standard work must be periodically revisited for relevance to both the current and desired future states.

At your next team offsite, I strongly recommend you build your team's leader standard work. Specify emphasis and proportions for each item and team member, and cascade leader standard work throughout the organization.

TCMI

As you'll notice, Teach, Coach, Mentor, and Inspire (TCMI) sits at the top of the list in my leader standard work. Although the rank-order and effort spent on TCMI varies across leaders, I feel very strongly that all leaders should have a version of TCMI in their list. You may be asking why you need all four elements. The simple answer is that three of the TCMI elements are tools for different aspects of your leadership obligations, and one is an outcome. Let's start with the outcome—inspire.

This is the most difficult element of the equation, because very few of us wake up in the morning and say, "I'm going to be inspirational today." Okay, if you're a motivational speaker, I suppose that's your job. But for the rest of us, inspiration can be fleeting and hard to pin down. There's also a big difference between being inspired and inspiring someone else—I argue that the latter is more difficult than the former. Also, although inspiration can come in an instant—like a lightbulb flickering on—inspiring another human in a management setting typically results from an accumulation of interactions and experiences.

Carl didn't inspire me the first day I met him in July of 1989, but I was impressed and a bit intimidated. It was only after witnessing, over time, his work ethic, ability to synthesize the complex into the understandable, and unflappable nature that I could say I was inspired to change my behavior and adopt many of his positive attributes as my own. You might be tempted to drop inspiration from your list of standard work, but I recommend you don't. I find it helpful to ask myself periodically if my actions and deeds have had the potential to be inspirational to those around me. Thinking about this helps to keep me sharp; you never know when you've inspired someone. It's a very rare occasion that an individual will admit directly that you've inspired them.

The teach and coach components of TCMI are much more straightforward but no less important. Both are focused on the short-term and more immediate outcomes. With teaching, you are imparting information that you have to another person or group with the intended outcome of improving their knowledge of a specific subject.

Although coaching[10] is also intended to yield a more immediate result, its focus is slightly different. In a coaching conversation, you're typically trying to get the recipient to see something for themselves or reach an intended conclusion independently. For example, I would coach a coworker to engage in a challenging conversation with a peer in an effort to resolve conflict between the two parties. During the conversation, I might suggest various approaches to resolution, but I'm typically not directing

---

10. Please keep your mind open to accepting advice and counsel from individuals who are more junior than you in the organization. Too often, we close our ears to teammates who we believe can't add incrementally to our experience and knowledge.

the coachee[11] to act in a specific way or say a specific thing. You engage in coaching when you see the potential for development and attempt to draw the intended result out of the coachee.

I like to employ professional coaches in circumstances where a subordinate is exhibiting challenging behavior that's out of the norm, is not gelling with the team, or has potential that's not being realized. Before I hire and assign a coach to a team member, I check two boxes. First, I decide that the coachee has the *potential* to change and will likely be *receptive* to change. Second, I see clearly that I personally can't spend the requisite amount of time doing the coaching, lack the specific coaching expertise needed for the situation, or see that the coachee would benefit from talking to an independent third party.

To be clear, it might appear on the surface that a coaching assignment is a bad thing, but it's quite the opposite. If I ask a subordinate to engage in a professional coaching regimen, it means that I care about the individual and the outcome. It means that I want to build the individual up and transfer learning back into the workplace. If the goal is to part ways, there are more expedient and cost-effective ways to do so.

Hopefully, you can see from my example about Carl that mentorship is special. Unlike teaching and coaching, which are short term and results focused, mentorship is long term and relationship based. In my own personal experience, all of my mentors were unplanned (with the exception of my parents—but who knows, maybe that was unplanned too!). I have been asked to be a mentor, but planned mentorship assignments rarely feel like mentorship in the moment. While I believe my interactions with planned mentees have provided value to both sides, in retrospect,

---

11. And yes, I know, *coachee* isn't technically a real word—at least not in this context—but it should be, and I'm not one to resist using a word that helps demonstrate my point just because it technically means "an American carriage shaped like a coach but longer and open in front," according to Merriam-Webster.

they were more like a series of coaching sessions. Teaching and coaching become mentorship with the benefit of time and the development of a strong relationship. That's why mentorship is so special. We've all had many teachers and/or coaches. However, I would wager you can count the number of mentors you've had on one, *maybe* two hands.

Before we leave the subject of mentorship, I'd like to indicate the characteristics that I believe are necessary for a successful mentor-mentee relationship. The mentee should "look up" to the mentor. Typically, the mentor is older and has more accumulated experiences to draw upon in the relationship. In my opinion, though, age is not a necessary condition. Like with coaching, the mentee should have an open mind (or at least have the door open a crack) and be receptive to new ideas and new ways of thinking. When Carl and I were in our heyday, I was extremely motivated to provide for Linda and our young family, so I soaked up his knowledge and experience like a sponge.

Mentors should be emotionally intelligent, be willing and able to simultaneously play the roles of cheerleader and constructive critic, and have the ability to be vulnerable at the appropriate times. It's essential that mentees know that the mentor is fallible and can make mistakes. What the mentee needs to learn is that it's okay to be vulnerable; it's okay to fall down. An excellent mentor shows the mentee how to learn and grow from challenges and mistakes. It's not the mistake that defines you—it's how you respond.

The Half Halt and Your Emotional Quotient

Recently, I woke up on the wrong side of the bed. A few bad dreams, an extremely early flight, concern over a few dropped balls . . . you know the drill.

A previous version of myself would have gone through the day with an extra crease between my eyebrows, my introversion taking over to limit communication with the outside world until I selfishly "worked through" my funk—on my terms. I was typically oblivious to how my mood was impacting those around me.

I've learned (mostly the hard way) that I'm in control of my mood. Although the circumstances that contributed to my current state may be outside of my direct control, the one thing I absolutely have control over is how I respond and how I move forward. I believe that the people around me genuinely care about my well-being and want to help me wrestle with my personal challenges. However, their ability and tolerance to do so is limited by their own baggage, bad dreams, early flights, and dropped balls.

Linda is an equestrian and competes at an advanced level in the art of dressage.[12] In dressage, there is the concept of a half halt, where the rider performs a nearly imperceptible collection move to prepare for the next part of the routine. The half halt is designed so that horse and rider can "take a breath" to rebalance and properly transition from one movement to the next. It's important to note that the routine doesn't stop. To the untrained eye (like mine), one would hardly notice that a half halt has occurred.

We could all learn from the half halt. Most of us live in a nonstop world—spaces and places where we get to truly stop, smell roses, and breathe are few and far between. The train keeps moving and rarely stops to let us on and off—we need tools like the half halt to help us collect and reflect while still moving forward.

So that morning when I woke up on the wrong side of the bed, I did a half halt between calls on the drive to the airport as a reminder that *I'm* the one who's in control of my mood, and that the people around me need me to be focused, positive, and in control. I want to give more than I take

---

12. Sometimes referred to as a "horse ballet," dressage is both a sport and an art form, where riders compete in dancelike performances atop their horses, synchronized to music. Dressage is an Olympic sport with roots that date back to the Roman Empire.

in this life, and the half halt construct has helped immensely to improve my emotional quotient and situational awareness. I'm not perfect by any measure, but by using a half halt I'm able to more clearly see the impact my mood is having on others and adjust more quickly.

If you'll indulge me with a brief aside, most people have never heard of dressage. Of those who have, many would describe it as being as exciting as watching paint dry. In reality, it's quite an extraordinary sport. Watching Linda improve over the years has taught me valuable lessons in persistence, tenacity, patience, and relationships. Imagine having a partner who can only understand your communication cues through gentle, tactile movements. Now imagine if your golf clubs or tennis racket had a mind of their own!

The concept is similar in business—you're constantly working with imperfect information and need to produce results by working with teams composed of humans who look, think, and feel differently than you do. The best teams are populated by individuals from different backgrounds, cultures, and geographies. As a leader, you attempt to create clarity through communication that gets interpreted differently by nearly everyone on the team. This inconsistency in interpretation forces you to repeat yourself to the point of being uncomfortable and to listen in ways that you never thought you'd have to in order to create harmony, balance, and understanding.

Part of your leader standard work should include creating your own version of the half halt. Remember that our job in this life is to give more than we take. Having the ability to self-correct mood and demeanor quickly, while the horse is still moving, will help improve your emotional quotient and situational awareness. Having a keen sense of *you* is half the battle.

The Distracted Workforce

In early April 2019, I was attending an EdTech conference in San Diego, California. Most of my time at this conference was spent "speed dating" with potential partners and vendors, but I made it a point to attend a few of the sessions—especially those with a focus on corporate education.

On the second day of the conference, I attended my first session, anticipating a robust conversation between the panelists. The room had a capacity of around two hundred, and roughly half of the seats were filled. When the lights dimmed and the session began, I turned to see the reaction of the room. Almost without exception, however, I found that participants were looking down at their phones and tablets—paying no attention to the engaging conversation that was happening on stage.

As a performer, teacher, and presenter, I'm acutely aware when an audience is in tune with the performance and when I've lost them. Typically, an audience will give you a chance before tuning out. This audience was distracted from the outset. The topic was interesting, and the panelists were doing a good job. Unfortunately, the audience was AWOL—each individual engrossed in their own world as the moderator and panelists spoke to what amounted to a handful of interested people.

For me, the worst part of this experience was that while I was mentally berating the audience for not paying attention, I was also subconsciously reaching for my own device. Once I realized what was happening, I worked to resist the urge to be rude and check my email. Ultimately, I put my hand into my suit coat and pulled out that blasted little ball and chain. Sure enough, the world hadn't ended in the ten minutes since the last time I'd checked, but there was a high pollen alert for my hometown (1,500 miles away) that I was glad to receive!

Back in La Crosse, three afternoons a week, I carve out an hour for a workout to clear my head and get centered. Having turned the corner on the second half of my life span, I have to balance the robustness of my routine with what my body can handle.[13]

One of my exercise routines is to briskly walk up and down the stairs in our six-story office building to get my heart rate up while minimizing wear and tear on my major joints. During a recent pre-COVID workout, a young woman from the building's cleaning company was cleaning the stairwell. She had a broom in both hands, and her mobile phone was glued to her ear—you know that precarious positioning where you're using your shoulder to keep the phone at your ear? For the first ten minutes, she was sweeping and talking to a friend, which is a wildly inefficient way to sweep a stairwell. At minute fifteen she was parked on the landing of the fourth floor texting with someone. At minute twenty-five she was almost to the second floor and back on the phone having another conversation. As my workout ended, she was at the bottom, taking another texting break.

Never mind that a broom is the wrong tool for the job. (As I took my final "lap," I noticed all the dust bunnies she'd missed and the chunks of dirt that remained in the stairwell.) Not only did the job take twice as long to complete as it should have, but it was also done poorly.

Distraction has been a problem in the meeting room for as long as there have been meetings. In the BCE (before cellphone era), distraction was easy to spot because Bill had a blank look on his face, Susan was staring out the window, and John's foot was tapping out the rhythm of morse code for the words "Help me!"

Modern distraction is, in my opinion, much worse. Today, a team meeting is typically populated by a combination of remote employees attending via video and individuals who are physically in the room. Let's temporarily ignore the challenges that the remote versus physical location em-

---

13. If you're reading this at age twenty-five or thirty, enjoy your current ability to do anything you want whenever you want without your body going into full revolt.

ployee dynamic creates in the conference room. Instead, let's focus on distraction.

Unlike the BCE days, when daydreaming was the primary method of escape, with modern devices you can transport yourself into another conversation entirely. If I pick up my phone in the middle of a meeting to respond to an instant message or email alert, I might as well have gotten up out of my chair and left the room. Instead of actively listening or physically engaging in the meeting, once I pick up my device, I'm transported somewhere else—into another conversation, my fantasy football league, or a gripping video of a neighbor's cat dressed up as Winston Churchill on social media.

Whatever it is that is most likely to grab your attention, a number of multibillion-dollar tech companies have created algorithms and artificial intelligence tools to sniff it out and put it in front of your eyes at the exact right moment. Your phone is essentially a collection of software applications designed to pull you out of reality and into the digital world for as long as possible. Our attention spans hardly stand a chance.

Worse yet, when you pick up your phone, it's highly likely that others in the room will follow suit. At a recent senior team offsite, I declared that everyone was to put their devices aside so we could minimize distractions. This "honor system" worked pretty well during day one, but midmorning on day two, a team member broke down and picked up his phone. Within seconds, another team member picked up her phone, and then there was a third.

These device "chain reactions" are common in the workplace, and I'm sure you've seen it happen. It's happened to you. It's happened to me. The problem is that this behavior lives in the subconscious mind. When you engage in distracting behavior with your device, it's almost assured that your poor choice will cascade to other team members and significantly alter meeting productivity and any positive team dynamic that existed before you pulled out your phone.[14]

I'm guilty. I'm guilty of starting chain reactions. I'm guilty of devicing (yes, I used it as a verb) during meetings. Heck, I'm guilty of believing that I needed to check my device at the dinner table with family and friends. I'm also appreciative that people in my life have cared enough to call me out on my behavior so I can be more aware and work to change my habits. A good first step in my rehabilitation is to think about how rude I'm being to family, friends, and colleagues when I check out. I should be present instead.

This concept of presence is the point. If I check my device during a meeting, I'm neither here nor there. When I'm at dinner and pick up my phone, I might as well be somewhere else. I'm clearly no longer engaged in the conversation, can't contribute, and am certainly not actively listening.

When I was mentally berating the audience at the conference, I was asking myself, "Why are they here?" Every person in the room had paid a lot of money to be there and was deriving little to no value from their attendance at that particular session. The continuous improvement expert in me was calculating all the waste that was being generated that afternoon. I'm sure there were employers who sent team members to the conference to learn and grow, but this was not the outcome of the session I attended.

When we're "multitasking" in meetings, we're not adding value to the meeting and we're not adding value to the business. In fact, corporate value is likely lost or possibly destroyed because the team missed an op-

---

14. There are many studies on device addiction and how technology is messing with our natural reward systems. According to a study published in the Harvard Business Review by Kristen Duke, Adrian Ward, Ayelet Gneezy, and Maarten Bos, "Merely having their smartphones out on the desk led to a small but statistically significant impairment of individuals' cognitive capacity—on par with effects of lacking sleep." In addition, Anderson Cooper and the CBS team at *60 Minutes* presented a fascinating piece on this subject called *Brain Hacking* that is a must-see.

portunity to come up with a unique solution to a challenge or a new way to go to market.

After thinking deeply about this subject, I realize that I've been failing my teams in the "help teams focus" category of my leader standard work. My behavior in team meetings and one-on-ones (1:1) with direct reports has been less than conducive to creating an environment of meaningful focus. I have not been as present as I should be and have instead been working under the erroneous assumption that I possess the mental agility to "context switch"[15] much more often than I can or should. My behavior sets the tone for the organization, and I have been inadvertently promoting the idea that multitasking is productive and creates a healthy organizational dynamic (which it does not).

So what can we do to bring ourselves and our teams back toward the center and create a more focused and productive work environment?

- Stop promoting the instant-response culture that our always-on tech tools have created and that we've taken advantage of. Unfortunately, this behavior has deeply affected our children. In fact, teens and young adults believe they're going to be pushed out of social groups if they don't immediately respond. I see this same behavior in adults. Sleep suffers, and concentration is challenged. Let's stop laying on the guilt (both directed and self-inflicted) if we don't immediately respond. Recall from part 3 that responsiveness does not mean an instant response is necessary.

- Minimize the alerts you receive on your phone. I have friends and coworkers who have their phones set to vibrate or ding every time they get an email, text message, news alert, or social media update. This feature may work for you, but have you thought about how distracting it is for your coworker in

---

15. *Context switching* started as a computing term for multithreaded machines but is now being adopted in business to describe the difficulty humans have jumping from one project or job to another.

the next cubicle to hear your phone go "ding" all day? Do we really need to know instantaneously when an email hits our inbox? If someone is breaking into my house, then I want an alert. During a meeting, do I really need to know that Jim's not showing up at dinner?

- Quarantine devices during meetings. State up front that your meeting will have a "no devicing" policy and that, at a minimum, devices need to stay out of reach (in a bag or coat pocket). As a compromise, take short "devicing breaks" every twenty to thirty minutes to allow team members to be sure their world hasn't imploded. Take these breaks under the guise of "stretch" or "cognitive load" breaks—which are good for all team members. There's plenty of scientific research that says sitting too long isn't healthy[16] and that cognitive load needs to be managed for best learning results.[17]

I'm sure there's more we should be doing to reduce distraction in the workplace, but the three suggestions above are meaningful and within our direct control. I've pledged to my teams that I'll be thinking more actively about my behavior in meetings and when we're in our one-on-one sessions. I've pledged to Linda that I'll work to be a better listener and be more present. Change will be difficult, and I won't be perfect, but I will try. Yes, this is the point where Yoda is ringing in my ears, "Do or do not. There is no try." Sorry, Yoda—this is a case where small, incremental improvement will win the day for me.

Have you ever given your device to someone else—even a close friend—to look at that cool picture you just took? I bet you've encountered feelings of apprehension at best and jealousy or anger at worst when your device was not returned expeditiously to your immediate control. This should

---

16. *Too Much Sitting: The Population-Health Science of Sedentary Behavior* by Neville Owen, Geneviève Healy, Charles E. Matthews, and David W. Dunstan, July 2010: US National Library of Medicine, National Institutes of Health.

17. For information on managing cognitive load in a learning environment, see *Efficiency in Learning: Evidence-Based Guidelines to Manage Cognitive Load* (2006) by Ruth Colvin Clark, Frank Nguyen, and John Sweller; Pfeiffer.

punch the point that the psychological and physical challenges of device distraction are real and pervasive.[18]

Being aware of the negative effects that device chain reactions can cause is half the battle. Let's be brave and let those closest to us know how it makes us feel when they check out at dinner. I'm certainly appreciative that I've been told how I make people feel when I check my email midconversation.

Let's all work on being more present in our work and at home . . . Wait, squirrel!

A Thought Experiment for a Healthy Team

If developing a healthy organization is a key priority for your business, congratulations! By now you realize that whatever stage of the journey your business is at, the work is both challenging and rewarding. You recognize that clear and frequent communication, clarity of vision and goals, agreement on a set of shared workplace behaviors, and the development of high-functioning teams are essential ingredients to success.

If you've made it this far and are confident in the health of your team, I recommend you take on the following challenge.

Here's the picture—you're the leader of your organization, and you've just won the lottery. You decide to spend your time writing the great American novel and traveling the world, leaving your team to decide what to do next. The board of directors has initiated a job search for your replacement, and after a period of chaos in the wake of your departure, the new chief executive has arrived on the scene. One by one, she calls the company's senior executives into her office to evaluate the situation and asks

---

18. Every Sunday morning, Apple sends me a usage report for the previous week. I'm frequently astonished that I spend an average of two-plus hours on my phone per day, and I'm an outlier on the low side of the distribution!

the following question, "Now that your former boss is gone, please provide me a list of three things you'd like to see changed in the company."

As a leader driving organizational health, you were probably respected by your team and generally liked throughout the company. However, human nature dictates that your former team members will jump at the chance to list all the things they would have changed or done differently during your tenure. In all relationships, things get left unsaid or some topics just seem too hard to address—strategy fatigue sets in. We rarely engage in this kind of hard work in the moment, but when the obstacle of your presence is removed, most former colleagues eagerly give a lengthy postmortem on the positives and negatives of the experience under your management. The answer typically goes something like, "Bill was a really nice guy, but I would have done _____," "_____ should have been a priority," or "Bill drove us nuts with _____."

Your assignment is to keep a three-hour slot open on the agenda at your next team offsite labeled "Team Thought Experiment" or something innocuous so as to not raise eyebrows. At the outset of this session, congratulate the team for all the hard work they've put in to establish a healthy team environment. Then state that the next few hours will likely be a test of that work. After this setup, pass out to each team member a single sheet of paper with a statement at the top that looks something like the following:

"If, hypothetically, I won the lottery tomorrow, what three things would you tell the new CEO or Board of Directors after my departure that you would have done differently during my tenure? Focus your attention on strategic business problems and not personnel issues or personality conflicts."

After a brief discussion to ensure everyone understands the assignment, give the group fifteen minutes to work independently on their answers.

When the team is done, call them back together and provide each team member the opportunity to present their ideas for five to ten minutes, leaving a few minutes for questions. At the end of the presentations, take a break and come back together to rank-order the best recommendations. Once you've rank-ordered the ideas, pick the top three from the list, grab some blank A3s,[19] and start solutioning![20]

---

19. Named after the size of the single sheet of paper used in the exercise, "A3" is a process for high-level planning as part of the Lean methodology. In brief, the process begins by identifying a problem at the top of a page, drawing or writing out a brief description of its current state, drawing or writing out a description of a desired future state, and filling in a number of standard sections to bridge the two. Those sections can include the challenges associated with reaching that future state, a root cause analysis to better define the problem, a dissection of the reasons behind the effort, a plan for implementation, benchmarks for success, and a follow-up plan. I encourage you to explore the process further at www.lean.org

20. Beware—this exercise should only be used with teams that are already pretty far along on an organizational health/continuous improvement journey.

PART 7
Leading Through Times of Crisis

The last existential threat to most businesses was born from economic greed and hubris prior to the Great Recession. If you were a leader in 2008, you were busy picking up the pieces from the devastation wrought by the impact that overextended, irresponsible, and in some cases criminal financial positions had on our economy.[1] As we began to slowly turn the economic corner in 2010, the leaders left standing showed incredible resilience and courage in the face of adversity. They metaphorically ran toward the fire, not away. They exhibited agility and worked with *purpose*. Many business leaders learned that organizational purpose would become a vaccine to help prevent hubris and greed from overtaking us again.

My personal journey as an executive leader began in the fires of the Great Recession. I had developed leadership experience over the twenty years preceding that event, but jumped into the deep end of the pool in 2008.

---

1.   "35 bankers were sent to prison for financial crisis crimes," Chris Isidore, April 28, 2016: CNN Money.

I was never one to run toward a fire, but in 2008 the very existence of Kaplan Professional (KP) and the company I had helped build—the Schweser Study Program for the CFA Exams—was in jeopardy. I just couldn't imagine a world without KP or Schweser. So I poured everything I had into ensuring the company's demise would not occur under my watch. I cared too deeply about the people, the clients, and the outcomes to do anything but succeed.

The current crisis we're living through as I write this in 2020 is quite different from the one that sparked the Great Recession. The current threat is unseen and insidious. Societal and personal anxiety are running high. Many social/societal norms and consumer consumption patterns will be permanently and substantially altered. Decision making is either paralyzed or inhibited by the opaqueness and uncertainty surrounding the "new world order" that will emerge.

Our leaders, and our leadership capabilities, are being tested as never before. The post-COVID-19 new world order is still highly uncertain, but companies that have established organizational trust and operate within a management operating structure of continuous improvement and organizational health will likely fare better than their counterparts who operate in an environment of ill-defined processes and organizational suspicion.

Those that make it out of the current crisis relatively unscathed will be labeled "lucky," but if you've been reading carefully, you know that luck has little to do with it. Being agile, maintaining strong alignment, championing effective communication and empathy, celebrating the diversity of your people, providing them with coaching and mentorship, encouraging them to bring their whole selves to work, and making a concerted effort to chip away at the clay layer will put companies in a much better position to evolve, pivot, and thrive in the face of current and future disruptions.

The pandemic will highlight those who were caught flat-footed and those who were up to the challenge, but it shouldn't take a global catastrophe for leaders to focus on nurturing a strong and healthy workplace culture. It is my hope that through this book, you've learned how to become a better leader, follower, employee, and all-around person and that those lessons will help guide you through whatever comes next in this fast-moving, chaotic, quickly changing pale blue dot of ours.

Running Toward the Fire

Author and leadership expert Robin Sharma once wrote, "Anyone can show exceptional leadership ability in easy times. When all's going to plan, anyone can be inspirational/excellent/innovative and strong. The real question is how do you show up when everything's falling apart?"[2]

While I argue with the assertion that "anyone" can show exceptional leadership when it's smooth sailing, the part of the quote that's relevant here is "how do you show up when everything's falling apart?"

Leading others is both a responsibility and a privilege. We accomplish what we do through others—our role is to direct, to support, and to care. That last point is crucial. We don't have to be friends with everyone we lead or even get along with them, but we must care about them.

Empathy and care are wonderful counterbalancing devices for leaders. If we treat the business as a machine, with inputs and outputs, people become coin-operated levers we pull to increase or decrease output and efficiency. Empathy and care allow leaders to walk in their team members' shoes and see the operations of the business through a different lens. Injecting the right levels of empathy and care into your management operating system will facilitate a different and more complete view of the company's most valuable asset—its people.

---

2. "Robin S. Sharma Quotes." BrainyQuote.com. BrainyMedia Inc, 2020. 9 October 2020. https://www.brainyquote.com/quotes/robin_s_sharma_628771

The key word is *balance*. Leaders must find the right balance between viewing the business as a complex system to be built, maintained, measured, and monitored with viewing the business as a collection of human interactions that must be nurtured and developed.

Putting people first does not mean there is an immutable contract to protect people and families at all cost. Sometimes, difficult employment decisions must be made to protect the business. Putting people first means you will consider the human element of your business as the primary ingredient to success and appropriately balance cold calculation with the realities of families and livelihoods.

I developed the mindset of a steward very early in my career. Growing up nurturing my own business and then extending that experience within the eighty-two-year legacy that Stanley Kaplan left for us has only served to strengthen that view.

Being a steward of the business means that I'm always balancing what's good for the company today with what will help the company thrive for another eighty-two years. Looking through a lens that extends that far in time gives me a true sense of stewardship. It makes the job less about me and more about the current and future generations that will follow. If we get it right, what we do today will positively affect families and investors for decades to come.

The danger of acting with a steward's mindset is that carrying the weight of future generations can lead to indecision and groupthink that slows the business down. It doesn't need to be that way. Surround yourself with good people, and act with strength and the resolve to do what's right for the current state, with a clear vision for the future—even when the decision-making waters get murky.

I also recommend keeping an old Mike Tyson quote in mind during times of crisis, "Everyone has a plan until you get punched in the mouth."[3] The best-laid plans get tossed out the window with alarming rapidity as the waters get more turbulent. I've seen many leaders succumb to their unwavering commitment to previously laid plans that are no longer relevant.

My view is that ego is the enemy of agility and creativity. Only when you set the ego aside can you truly see what's possible. When the ego is quiet, the ears hear more, and the mind makes connections that seemed impossible when the ego was active.

This may sound quaint, but breathing and meditation in appropriate doses do wonders to calm the ego—especially if you focus on the little things you're grateful for while quieting your mind.

During times of heightened stress, you may find yourself dodging unfamiliar arrows and barbs. These barbs may come in unexpected forms and from unusual directions. External competition may become more fierce, and you may find team members are more vigorously protecting their territory and authority. Be the leader who sees the bigger picture. Help others see connection points and collaboration opportunities that break down unnecessary politics and protectionism.

A crisis is a wonderful time to thaw organizational permafrost and tap into veins of discretionary effort that are locked in the clay layer of disengaged middle management. Show others that by working together, your organization will prevail. Championing new, collaborative approaches to management will test your courage and resilience. You will be uncomfort-

---

3. Tyson explained the meaning behind that quote in a 2012 story by Mike Berardino in the *South Florida Sun Sentinel*. "If you're good and your plan is working, somewhere during the duration of that, the outcome of that event you're involved in, you're going to get the wrath, the bad end of the stick," he's quoted as saying. "Let's see how you deal with it. Normally people don't deal with it that well."

able. But remember, we only grow by being placed into uncomfortable situations.[4]

Being in a leadership role is like being on stage, where every expression and move you make is magnified. In times of crisis, this magnification is amplified even further. Our teams will read a great deal into our demeanor and tone of voice. Leaders must be calm, persistent, and thoughtful.

Let's return to the first paragraph of this part; the most important thing a leader should model is the *purpose* of the organization. Leaders must live the cause. They must be in the center of the fight. I'm incredibly fortunate to know clearly the purpose of our organization, and I work to model it each day.

As advised previously, say things seven times (or more) to get your message across as communication often breaks down in times of crisis. Rumor and innuendo travel like wildfire as stress levels rise. During times of crisis, clear, frequent, and consistent communication is more important than ever.

When I use the word *consistent*, I'm not implying that the content of the message doesn't change. The message may need to change frequently during a crisis, but the lines of communication should remain as open as possible. Part of your communication regimen should include coaching teams and team members about the need for agility, flexibility, and creativity at all levels of the company.

I will certainly emerge from this crisis a changed man. I believe we will all be affected in a meaningful way. The choice you have is this: You can passively allow the crisis and all its negativity to impact you. You can run from the fire and hope for an eventual return to the normal you once knew.

---

4. "Learning Is Supposed to Feel Uncomfortable," Peter Bregman, August 21, 2019: HBR.org.

Alternatively, you can use the crisis as an opportunity to build skills, add to your tool kit, and run toward the fire. You can push the bounds of your creativity and agility to develop new ways of thinking and being. You can embrace change and help influence the new world order that emerges from the ashes of economic, political, and societal upheaval.

I'll finish this section with a quote from Warren Buffett, "Only when the tide goes out do you discover who's been swimming naked."[5] Here in 2020, the tide is receding at an unprecedented rate. I'm confident that if you commit to growing the leadership qualities outlined above, you and your organization will be capable of weathering the storm ahead and emerge fully clothed.

COVID-19 and the Social Norm of Powering Through

I'd like to extend an open apology to everyone I've ever infected by venturing out of the house with a cold or flu in the past. Like many in our society, when I got sick, I'd load up on over-the-counter meds and power through. Powering through is expected. It is the norm, but it's one we have to break.

On a Sunday morning in early March 2020, at a time when there were only a handful of known COVID-19 cases in the country, I found myself in a fever-induced daze, recovering from a bout with what I suspected was the flu—testing was not yet available, and to this day, I have no idea whether or not I was infected with COVID-19. In that moment, however, it hit me how incredibly selfish I've been in the past to venture out in public when I've known, or should have known, I was contagious.

I lay there listening to the latest COVID-19 rumblings on TV, thinking about all the meetings, dinners, and events I've attended while under the weather. "Was my presence at Tuesday's staff meeting so important that

---

5.   "Swimming Naked When the Tide Goes Out," *Time* staff, April 2, 2009: Money.com.

the risk of infecting others was outweighed by my contributions? Did my attendance make or break the fund-raising gala I was convinced I had to attend?"

The answer is a resounding no. If I infect even one person, I infect that person's family. I potentially infect their friends and colleagues, some of whom might be more susceptible to the potential damage an illness can cause. My choice to show up when I'm contagious negatively impacts the productivity of many other people and inappropriately puts them at risk. How do I know if Billy in accounting is immunocompromised? How do I know if Sally has her grandmother living in the basement with lung disease? I don't.

If you're not convinced that your performance isn't what you think it is when you power through, I've got news for you. On that Sunday morning during my fuzzy fever time, I did a little work on our personal taxes to try to stay productive. I thought I was making reasonable headway, just moving a bit slower than normal. The process culminated with my getting several IRS forms ready to pop in the mail the next day.

I woke up the following morning to discover my fever had broken overnight. My wife, Linda, brought me the envelopes I'd prepared the day before and asked me to look at them. After a few moments of getting oriented, I realized I had put the stamps in the upper *left* corner! I then had to open each envelope, review the forms for errors and repackage everything. What a waste of effort.

The lesson is that even though you think you're being productive when you power through, the probability of making mistakes rises. I'd have been better off spending my downtime playing another game of Scrabble® against the computer.

We're coached from a young age to power through. We strive for that perfect attendance record. We're told to sacrifice for the team. "Suck it up, buttercup" is a common refrain. Illness is viewed as a sign of weakness, and we go to extraordinary lengths to cover it up when we're sick. We are bombarded with advertising by over-the-counter pharmaceutical manufacturers that attempt to convince us to consume Product X, and our symptoms will be sufficiently masked so we can get right back to our routines.

The implication of these messages is that all that matters is *you*—that *you* feel okay and are back in the game as quickly as possible. There isn't nearly enough emphasis on ensuring you're no longer in transmission mode when you re-enter your social circles.

Now, let's extend the argument against powering through to our interconnected world. The global economy is built on social mobility and interconnectedness. Trade, entertainment, travel, education—almost every aspect of our economy depends upon the free flow of goods and ideas. Human interactions and experiences are essential to how we view the world.

Although there are some individuals who would like nothing more than to close borders and return to a less connected and less diverse time, I believe such a regressive step would be tragic for all of us who live on this unique, pale blue dot. We mustn't succumb to paranoia and retreat into the past.

However, with the interconnectedness of the modern world comes the heightened risk of new biological threats. We can no longer blissfully imagine we're somehow immune to the threat or think there won't be another pandemic after COVID-19 fades into the rearview mirror of our collective consciousness.

We have an obligation as citizens to change how we think about the norm of powering through. I believe we can make an impact by changing our viewpoints and behavior as follows:

1. Use sick days for their intended purpose. As a leader, I can't tell you how frustrated I get when I hear colleagues or neighbors tell me with a wink that they're using a sick day to recover from a long party weekend. Then, when the real thing comes along, the individual has burned through their bank of allotted sick days, powers through, and infects the whole office. On the flipside, there are those who wear the fact that they haven't taken a sick day in years as a badge of honor. Here, the result is the same—they feel their presence is so important that it's worth the risk of infecting others.

2. Ensure cross-training and coverage for your role. Many people power through because there isn't proper cross-training or coverage for their role if they *do* get sick. It's management's responsibility to help team members feel safe enough to take sick days when they need to.

3. Even if you're like me and prefer to work in an office environment, make sure you're set up to be productive working from home. One fortunate outcome of the COVID-19 pandemic is that working from home has become more ubiquitous and acceptable. Those who are set up to work remotely won't have to struggle with the decision of whether to show up to work when they could potentially infect others, because they can be just as effective from home.

4. Be proactive about your health. Do what your mother told you to do—exercise, eat right, and sleep. Eliminate excess stress from your life, and take stock of potentially unhealthy influences on your body's defenses. Being active and engaging in a healthy lifestyle help promote a stronger immune system. That stronger immune system will come in handy when cold and flu season comes around.

If there's a benefit to the global challenges faced as a result of COVID-19, it's that many of us will have a heightened awareness of how disease is transmitted and will be more in tune with our personal role in its spread. We won't be able to completely prevent the spread of disease and illness. However, being more aware of our own impact on those around us, and actively working to break down the norm of powering through, will go a long way toward keeping us all safe.

Lead by example. Show others that you take their well-being seriously by staying home when you're ill. Sometimes you don't know you're contagious until it's too late, but I'm committed to being more careful in the future. I care about you and your family's well-being.

Organizational Trust and Returning to the Office after COVID-19

During the early phases of the pandemic, I had a socially distanced conversation with a friend about returning to work as the government began to ease Safer-at-Home orders.[6] She told me her company was recalling all employees back to the office who had been working from home since mid-March, effective the next week, which was in mid-May.

From previous conversations we'd had about her job and employer, I knew enough about the work she did to know that it was not essential for her to be on-site. Curious to understand the root cause of her leader's order to bring everyone back together so soon, I started asking the "five whys" from my Lean training.[7] Created by Toyota founder Sakichi Toyoda—who is often referred to as the Japanese Thomas Edison—the five whys are designed to get to the root of any problem. With each "why," the source or motivation of a problem or decision becomes more clear, and by the fifth "why," a solution is likely to emerge.

---

6. The name given to Wisconsin's social-distancing policies during the pandemic.
7. https://kanbanize.com/lean-management/improvement/5-whys-analysis-tool

My first question was, "Why are they bringing everyone back so soon?" To this, she indicated that the team was highly collaborative and handoffs between work streams were more efficient when everyone was physically together. To gain more clarity, I asked about her team's efficiency during their seven weeks of working from home. She replied that there had not been any challenges to getting work done in a timely manner and that some on her team felt they were more efficient than when they worked at the office.

I thought to myself, "Self, something else is going on here. The unknowns that surround the novel coronavirus[8] would lead me to keep as many people home for as long as possible if teams and individuals were able to be as, or more, productive than when they were in the office."

This seeming contradiction led me to my second "why." I asked, "If some teams are more productive working from home, why are they bringing everyone back and not limiting the first round to the factory and production personnel who are necessary to build and ship products to customers?"

Her reply this time was less confident, and I sensed a waver in her voice. "I guess they just want everyone back together to make sure all the work is getting done properly," she said.

"Ah . . . we're starting to get to the root cause," I thought to myself.

Then I turned the conversation to productivity measurement in a work-from-home environment. We discussed how, if you keep all else the same, it's hard to "hide" low productivity when working from home, because over time, subpar performers begin to stick out like a sore thumb relative to those who are more skilled and efficient. She agreed that unless there are known reasons why one individual's work-from-home experience should differ from another's (e.g., lack of proper work environment, uncontrol-

---

8. Remember, this occurred in mid-May 2020, just a few months after the first case of this new and mysterious virus was reported in the United States.

lable distractions, etc.), it would quickly become clear that a particular individual was not pulling their weight.

One more why . . . This time, I simply asked the question again: "Why do you think they want everyone back in the office?"

Her response? "I guess they don't trust us."

Throughout this book, I've written about the importance of organizational health and organizational trust. Myriad articles, books, and other publications speak to the subject of trust. A cottage consulting industry has been thriving on the subject for years.[9] Healthy organizations have been shown to perform better than their peers and exhibit higher levels of employee engagement and retention. Trust is a central component of any effective organizational health model.

Trust within a team and between colleagues is built over time and is a two-way street among peers, managers, and subordinates. For example, if Billie and I work together at different points along the value chain, trust is built with effective and consistent communication. Trust grows with high-quality handoffs that are repeatable and reliable. Trust builds when I admit failure to Billie, own my mistakes, and learn from challenges. If Billie falls down, she does the same.

With the right accountability, communication, and process-flow frameworks in place, trust should be the baseline assumption. If a teammate doesn't follow through or reliably deliver quality work, a culture of communication, accountability, and candor can shorten the climb back up the trust ladder. Clearly defined responsibility matrices (RACI) are also an essential ingredient in building organizational trust.

---

9. This includes those founded by some of the top authorities on the subject, such as Patrick Lencioni's *The Table Group* and Stephen M. R. Covey's *The Speed of Trust.*

Alternatively, if accountability, communication, responsibility matrices, and process-flow systems are not in place or are ineffective, organizational trust is much harder to establish.

In low-trust environments, processes live in people's heads and not on process maps. Communication happens around the water cooler, messages are twisted to serve individual interests, and no one knows who's on first, second, or third! Suspicion surrounding motives abounds, and *mistrust* becomes the baseline assumption between teams and team members. Even if everyone *wants* to trust each other, building trust is damn near impossible because a few steps up the trust ladder are negated when a process or communication failure occurs.

Now, transport yourself back to early March 2020. The novel coronavirus is just taking off, and businesses that can send employees to work from home have done so with only days of planning. Businesses that have established high levels of organizational trust are, in relative terms, much better off than those that have not. These organizations have invested in management training, employee engagement, process definition, and communication systems. They have clearly defined goals and have established responsibility matrices that align with their goals. They can measure productivity and have a good handle on customer satisfaction through rapid-feedback systems.[10] Trust is the baseline, and productivity/engagement is as high as possible given the circumstances.

Imagine for a moment the opposite. It's early March, and an unbalanced organization needs to send everyone home for an undetermined amount of time to ride out the storm. In this case, anxiety among both employees and managers runs high. Managers are freaking out because they have no idea what their people are doing minute by minute. They're accustomed to looking over their employees' shoulders to ensure the work gets done

---

10. This is typically done by using Net Promoter Score (NPS) or other similar customer feedback tools.

and manually intervening in process flow because of all the organizational uncertainty and system breakdowns. In this type of business, managers are fixers and overseers, not talent developers and coaches.

Similarly, employees are freaking out for all the obvious reasons: They've never worked from home before. There's a silent killer on the loose. Their kids are home from school. They've been thrust into substitute teacher roles. They're also freaking out because they've become accustomed to an unhealthy work environment where their every move is tracked and suspicion in people and systems runs rampant. What happens now?

In this environment, both parties want to get back to the physical office as quickly as possible so everyone can keep an eye out for problems, protect their jobs, and watch their backs.

If you're a leader who pushed to bring your teams back into the office as quickly as possible, ask yourself: Why did I rush? What were your motivations for pushing the envelope? Ask yourself as many "whys" as you need in order to arrive at the root cause of that decision. Allow your open mind to consider all possibilities.

If this exploration has led you to a place of vulnerability and the root cause centers around a lack of organizational trust, then begin working immediately to adopt the principles of continuous improvement and organizational health. There's no better time than the present to begin taking meaningful steps up the organizational trust ladder.

The post-COVID-19 new world order is still highly uncertain, at least at the time of this writing. However, companies that have established organizational trust and operate within a management operating structure of continuous improvement and organizational health will likely fare better than their counterparts who operate in an environment of ill-defined processes and organizational suspicion.

CONCLUSION:
Learning from Our Past

Where are your family pictures? If you're like many families, old photos collect dust in boxes or are relegated to photo albums that sit on a shelf in the den, only to be viewed on special occasions.

My wife, Linda, and I started the herculean task of scanning family memories several years ago and "finished" the project during the early stages of the COVID-19 pandemic. Once digitized, we updated the metadata on each photo to ensure dates and faces were properly categorized. Even with the best technology, it's a tedious task, but the job satisfaction realized upon completion is tremendous.

We've linked our Apple TV to the native Photos app on our iMac and enjoy a rotation of roughly 1,500 of our best memories on our living room television when the Apple TV goes into screensaver mode.[1]

---

[1] A quick PSA: You no longer need a clunky flatbed scanner to digitize your trove of family pictures. All you need is a good smartphone with a better than average camera and the PhotoScan by Google app.

I'm a history buff of sorts and am particularly enthralled by early European history.[2] I'm a firm believer that if we don't learn from our past, we are destined to repeat it. As a continuous improvement leader, I believe mistakes and errors are only failures if we refuse to use them as learning opportunities.

One evening while Linda and I were cleaning up after dinner, the TV went on screensaver mode and the family pictures began scrolling. I glanced up to see a wonderful family picture from 1997. Our sons Brandon and Nick were respectively six and four at the time, and we were standing in front of my in-laws' Christmas tree with big cheesy grins on our faces.

While looking at that photo, it dawned on me that I had questions for the version of myself that was staring back at me on the big screen:

- What was going on behind 1997 Andy's eyes?
- Was 1997 Andy the best possible version of himself in that moment?
- What were the challenges 1997 Andy faced?
- How did he approach solving those challenges?

As we sat down to resume our evening, my mind began to wander to questions I needed to ask the 2020 version of me:

- Do I like the person I remember from that picture? Was I doing my best to be a role model and a positive influence on those closest to me?
- What were my positive attributes in 1997?
- Have I let any of those positive attributes atrophy? How should I approach rebuilding those beneficial traits to influence the next best version of me?

---

2. If you're also into history and would like a reference to new material, I'll make a plug here for Jaime Jeffers's *British History* podcast.

- Did I learn from the pain that lay behind my eyes in that photo?

- Have I built a convenient, but not entirely honest, narrative of who I was at that point in my life?

- What else can I learn about that time that can help me improve today?

After that episode of self-reflection, my next epiphany was that although I'm a history buff, the history I tend to focus on is that of *other* people, times, and places. What about the rich collection of personal lessons we have at our fingertips? For many of us, that history is filed away on basement shelves and seldom revisited.

The pandemic and ensuing lockdown has slowed the world to a grinding halt and in doing so, has provided space for self-reflection. It's also forced each of us to face the consequences of our life's decisions. After all, when you're sheltering in place, there is no running from, hiding from, or ignoring problems that have been left unaddressed, pushed aside, or otherwise repressed.

Those with a fixed mindset and a narrow view will likely find themselves struggling a little harder than most during this period. They will feel the crushing weight of isolation much more acutely. Rather than taking the opportunity to do some self-reflection, they'll be extremely eager to return to the way things were as quickly as possible.

My hope is that through the practices outlined previously—such as meditation, self-reflection, the half halt, and continuous improvement—you will find the strength of character to take this opportunity to ask yourself some of the tough questions you may have been avoiding.

Time invested in bringing your memories out from their analog vaults is time well spent. The exercise of constructively reviewing your past can unlock opportunities for learning and growth that may have been long forgotten.

I'm not suggesting we get lost in constantly revisiting our past. Dwelling on our pain and challenges can be unhealthy if not done with an eye toward personal development and growth. It's likely that many of us will need the help of a third-party therapist or coach—I did. Likewise, stuffing our history into sealed boxes and only periodically reviewing the thin veneer of forced smiles for staged photos without diving deeper is, in my opinion, a wasted opportunity.

Digging into our past experiences with an eye toward learning and improving can help us identify opportunities to better ourselves and, by extension, to make better career choices, improve our social interactions, and strengthen relationships with our immediate family.

Hence, the starting point of any personal continuous improvement journey is understanding the self. Only after we've taken the necessary time to reflect, evaluate, and learn from our past can we begin repairing and improving our relationships with others.

Once we've asked ourselves these difficult questions, it's time to evaluate and reflect on our most intimate relationship. When Linda and I were preparing to get married for the first time in the mid-1980s, we sat down with the pastor who would eventually marry us and were asked a series of difficult questions—questions that I, in hindsight, couldn't really fully comprehend at the ripe old age of twenty-two. Although the questions were many, they essentially boiled down to one: is this *true love*, or just lust?

At my young age and relative level of experience, I couldn't really grasp the meaning behind the question. I didn't understand what "true love" meant at the time, nor how to evaluate my commitment to my relationship with Linda. As a result of COVID-19, many relationships are now being put to the same test. The lockdown has forced us to remain in place with our loved ones for long periods of time. The situation will likely serve to allow healthy, balanced relationships to grow stronger, but those built on a weak foundation (e.g., lust and/or convenience) will likely buckle under the pressure.

In hindsight, as we sat across from the pastor in early 1986, I wasn't fully ready to offer as much of myself to Linda as was necessary for a healthy union, but lacked the maturity and experience to recognize it at the time. Today, after all we've been through, I know we made the right choice to remarry in 2009 after our "great struggles" that began in late 2003. The pandemic has only further confirmed the choices we made.

After we've taken the necessary time to evaluate and repair ourselves and our relationship with our life partners, we can then turn our attention to our broader family units. Relationships between parents and children can be complicated and at times difficult. Like any other relationship, though, they require a high degree of trust, mutual respect, and balance. If those relationships were fraying prior to COVID-19 or if long-standing issues and differences were continually being swept under the rug, the countless hours together under lockdown will eventually bring them to the surface.

Throughout the summer of 2020, the market for personal recreational vehicles exploded; today, it's nearly impossible to find an available RV,[3] boat,[4] motorcycle/ATV,[5] or bicycle.[6] I fear that people are purchasing such items because they can offer an escape from their home life. It is my sincere hope that new toys are instead being used for shared activities and outings that can help bring families closer together. In any event,

---

3. "Pandemic pushes travelers to take to the road in RVs," by Robert Ferris, July 27, 2020: CNBC.com
4. "'Everyone is buying boats' during the pandemic, and it's causing a short supply," by Chris Woodyard, August 29, 2020: *USA Today*.
5. "The Pandemic Paradox: Motorcycle Sales Are Up," by Andrew Cherney, June 26, 2020: Cycleworld. com
6. "Thinking of Buying a Bike? Get Ready for a Very Long Wait," by Christina Goldbaum, May 18, 2020: *New York Times*.

families have been sheltering in place together for months at this point, with many more long months ahead. As with any relationship, that much togetherness can be difficult. However, we can all make our home lives a little more peaceful by framing the crisis as an opportunity to repair unresolved issues and grow closer as a family.

The first step toward that end is self-reflection. The next is to understand the lens through which each of our family members sees the world. Everyone in our households is likely struggling with the effects of the crisis in unique ways. In this environment, a little empathy and communication can go a long way in bringing families closer. Using your new motorcycle or boat as an avoidance mechanism will likely only serve to make things worse.

Let's expand our view a little further; the pandemic has also put our relationships with friends and communities to the test. Getting together has never been more difficult, inconvenient, or time consuming, and can even pose a threat to our health.[7] We've been forced to be more thoughtful about who we spend our time with and consider whether we're getting enough out of that interaction to make it worth the investment. In times of personal crisis, we often discover who our real friends are; in times of communal crisis, that effect is amplified.

Before the pandemic, I knew many people (myself included) who felt the need to have an active social schedule; humans are social creatures and are wired to seek the approval of others. FOMO, or the "fear of missing out," dictated many social calendars prior to the pandemic. We packed our weekends and evenings with events and outings. We cared deeply about how others viewed us. We felt the pressure of presenting the image of our best selves—not necessarily our *genuine* selves—to the outside world at all times. I hope this brief respite from the days of constant social

---

7. Online video platform-based "happy hours" and online gameplay have helped fill the void but are not direct substitutes for in-person human interaction.

interaction will provide an opportunity to reflect on the value of our relationships. Perhaps those that are most worth our time haven't been given appropriate energy and dedication in the past; perhaps more superficial relationships were prioritized too highly.

Many of us can't wait to return to our former social lives, but as things return to normal, I encourage you to consider whether you truly *want* to attend all of those events and social gatherings or if you're just doing it for some level of social approval. My hope is that in the new world order that emerges, we remain aware of who we choose to surround ourselves with and that we continue to constructively question the value of each relationship. I hope that we put more of ourselves into the relationships that are really worth the effort while being more comfortable letting go of those that aren't.

Finally, the pandemic has provided an opportunity for us to put into question our contribution to the world of work. In an ideal world, we've all found opportunities that align with our interests and abilities; in reality, that is often not the case. The clay layer exists in part because individuals often don't think carefully enough about the career choices they're making, or will purposely pursue a particular path for the wrong reasons. Sometimes careers are chosen because they can offer financial stability, appease parental or societal pressure, or follow some preconceived tradition and/or heritage. None of these are inherently bad reasons to pursue a particular path, but they can result in a career that doesn't align with one's interests and abilities.

The pandemic has offered us an opportunity to stop and reflect on those decisions. Use the five whys to get to the real reason why you do what you do. If you're less than satisfied with your true motivations, draw up an A3 that evaluates your current state of being, your desired future state, and the obstacles that stand in the way.[8] Use the COVID-19 transition as a unique moment in time to evaluate your inventory of skills, competencies, and capabilities. Then plan to pursue opportunities for further education in the areas that are lacking. Just imagine how much better off we'd be as a society if we all took this opportunity to learn one new skill or to do the difficult work of self-reflection and focus on personal continuous improvement.

The Final Act

Success without balance is often more disastrous than failure with balance.

When the unbalanced achieve victory, it often serves to further destructive habits. When the balanced suffer defeat, resilience and perseverance grow.

It takes a great deal of self-awareness, humility, emotional intelligence, curiosity, and balance to learn from failure. Those with a closed, unbalanced mind will blame others for their failures and, over time, will come to believe their own narratives as truth. If things work out, they want the credit; if things fall apart, it was the fault of some other person or team. The only way to learn, evolve, and grow is to face our failures head-on and learn from mistakes.

Don't get me wrong, it's a constant struggle—nobody has it perfectly figured out. However, reflecting on and learning from negative experiences is a necessary first step toward continuous improvement. Rather than blaming others for that failed relationship, failed product launch, or big sale that slipped through their fingers, those who are on a continuous improvement journey are better equipped to examine the root cause of

---

8. If you need a refresher on A3s, refer back to the detailed footnote near the end of part 6.

that failure and will evolve to become better prepared to face whatever challenges await them in the future.

Crises provide ample opportunity for self-reflection, introspection, and learning from our past. You might be reading these words in a period of relative calm. However, as we learned in 2020, 2008, 2001, and so on, calm is a fleeting, temporary condition. Our ability to weather future storms will be significantly improved if, moving forward, we embark on a continuous improvement journey that enables us to achieve greater balance in all aspects of our lives.

For now, I'll leave you with this: We all live in a state of imbalance—myself included. I've purposely written the stories in this book to remind *myself* to always strive for balance. Our subconscious minds work continually to help us correct and adjust as we move forward in our daily lives, but we rarely *make* the time to consciously contemplate how we can return to center. Becoming more aware of the balancing acts we constantly play will help us to be better colleagues, leaders, friends, and family members. Polarization, fixed mindsets, and operational silos are destructive to corporate value and damage relationships of all kinds. My aim is to elevate the concepts of self-awareness, mental agility, active listening, two-way communication, and bringing one's "whole self" to work to drive improved alignment and outcomes for both the organization and its people.

I'm glad you joined me on my personal journey to teach, coach, mentor, and inspire current and future leaders as we all work to find balance between strength and vulnerability, confidence and selflessness, passion and measure, single-mindedness and inclusivity, determination and curiosity, and leadership and followership.

Grace. Dignity. Compassion.